Matt Martinez, Jr.

and

Steve Pate

Doubleday

New York   London   Toronto   Sydney   Auckland

Matt Martinez's Culinary Frontier

A REAL TEXAS COOKBOOK

PUBLISHED BY DOUBLEDAY
a division of Bantam Doubleday Dell Publishing Group, Inc.
1540 Broadway, New York, New York 10036

DOUBLEDAY and the portrayal of an anchor with a dolphin are
trademarks of Doubleday, a division of Bantam Doubleday Dell
Publishing Group, Inc.

Book design by Jennifer Ann Daddio
Illustrations by Dorothy Reinhardt

Library of Congress Cataloging-in-Publication Data
Martinez, Matt, Jr.
Matt Martinez's culinary frontier : a real Texas cookbook / Matt
Martinez. Jr. and Steve Pate. — 1st ed.
p.   cm.
Includes index.
1. Cookery, American—Southwestern style.   2. Cookery—
Texas.   3. Mexican American cookery.   I. Pate, Steve.
II. Title.
TX715.2.S69M35   1997
641.59764—dc20
96-38407
CIP

This book is dedicated to Janie and Matt Martinez, Sr.,

parents of Matt Martinez, Jr. Their trials and

tribulations made everything possible.

A tenacious boxer in his early days, Big Matt

remains a fighter, but now against an invisible

opponent, Parkinson's disease.

Acknowledgments

The authors wish to thank the late Frank X. Tolbert and his legendary chili book, *A Bowl of Red*, which was first published by Doubleday in 1972, for details on the story about the Lady in Blue.

The authors are grateful for the support of all family and friends, particularly that of Matt's wife, Estella; his mother, Janie; and his uncle, David Gaytan. Also, for the helpful contributions of John Anders, Lizzie Ashworth, Jay Brousseau, Diana Coley, Denne Freeman, Ley Jaynes and Walter Walsh of Grailey's Fine Wines, Mike Jones, Bill Morgan, Jones Ramsey, Darrell Royal, Walter Robertson, Gina Schadt, the people at Servi Cigar, and Carlton and Pat Stowers.

We also wish to thank our most essential compadres in this effort: Judy Kern, our Doubleday editor; Janet Wilkens Manus, our agent; and Matt's loyal customers everywhere.

Contents

It troubles me that certain left-handed chefs, riding on the coattails of Southwestern cuisine, are getting away from the traditional, early Texas, and prairie-style recipes. This cookbook is the Real McCoy. This is the way cooking was done under a prairie sky, and how it's supposed to be. We're merely perfecting what was done right in the first place.

—MATT MARTINEZ, JR.

The Gospel of Cooking According to Matt

If my grandfather, Delfino Martinez, had not avoided his own hanging, my family would not exist. Nor would our restaurants. Or this cookbook.

I am eternally grateful for his elusiveness, as well as the shortcomings of his captors.

Delfino Martinez grew up in northern Mexico and, at age fourteen, joined Pancho Villa's army in the fight against the Federales in the Mexican Revolutionary War. By seventeen, he was a captain in Villa's army.

A few years later, the Federales captured Delfino near the Texas border town of Laredo. In that war, prisoners must have been a real nuisance, because no one wanted them hanging around—unless it was from a tree.

Some were indeed left dangling at the ends of rough ropes. Some were blindfolded and led before firing squads. And still others encountered even more creative means of being killed on the spot.

For some reason—and no one in my family is sure why or how—Delfino's execution was delayed. Instead, his wife received a telegram from the Mexican government. "We're hanging your husband tomorrow morning," the note promised. "If you want the body, bring a wagon."

A friendly messenger lurking outside the jail sent word to Delfino's faithful wife Maria to disregard the Federales' orders. Go instead, the messenger said, to Eagle Pass—another border town, a hundred miles northwest of Laredo.

This may or may not have been an easy decision for her, but I'm tickled to report that Grandma rode her wagon to Eagle Pass and waited. Fortunately for her—and, I should add, the rest of the Martinez family—Delfino showed up a few days later.

Nobody's alive to explain how my grandfather made his getaway. What I do know is that his new lease on life either gave him an appetite for cooking, or he had it all along. He and Maria eventually settled in Austin, Texas, and they began cooking what, many years later, would become known as Tex-Mex food.

At first, they set up a wagon right on the grounds of the Texas state Capitol and sold tortillas and the sweetest of praline candies to state dignitaries and others passing by the big dome.

By 1925, my grandparents had put together enough of a meager

Delfino Martinez and his wife, Maria; Matt Jr.'s paternal grandparents

Matt Martinez's Culinary Frontier

savings to open Austin's first Tex-Mex restaurant—named El Original (El O-ree-hee-nal). I suppose the love for cooking is deeply embedded in us, for in June 1952, Delfino's son, Matt Martinez, Sr., and his wife, Janie, opened the doors to Matt's El Rancho, which remains Austin's most popular Tex-Mex restaurant. Over the years, Matt and Janie made many, many tamales and tacos and enchiladas, and they also made four babies. I was the first, and the only boy.

In the early years, Matt's El Rancho was a small, crowded place on East First Street. Its charm stemmed from the fact that there was none; old chairs and tables were

Matt Sr. and his wife, Janie— their wedding portrait

practically jammed side by side. And they were always filled. My mother cooked in the back, while my father hawked customers off the streets. Dad would promise them, "If you don't like the food, you don't have to pay for it."

Most bellies were too full and most mouths were too busy for anyone to be asking for their money back.

My father was a billboard on shoes, a walking advertisement. He also served as maître d', publicity director, marketing director, chief of finance, and whatever other hat had to be worn that particular time of day.

Matt's El Rancho was so popular that my parents added on to the café four times. Then they bought the land across the street to build a bigger El Rancho.

A U.S. President (Lyndon Johnson), many Texas governors, sports and mystery writers, country humorists, guitar pickers and grinners, sports heroes, and politicians galore frequented the old Matt's El Rancho on First Street; and, most made an even later move to the current location on South Lamar, where the tradition continues in a 400-seat "mansion" that could have housed the old place in one of several dining rooms.

I grew up in the El Rancho kitchens of my mother and father, as well as the kitchen of my grandmother, Maria Gaytan, and a lot of other kitchens. The kitchen has always been my favorite room in the house.

In 1986, I opened my own restaurant in downtown Dallas at the Plaza of the Americas Hotel. That foothold eventually allowed me to open a Tex-Mex restaurant in East Dallas, and then I settled into the Lakewood area with Matt's Rancho Martinez. I later added Mattito's (since sold) in the Oak Lawn section of Dallas.

In 1993, I opened Matt's No Place next door to Rancho Martinez. No Place is my celebration of good ol' cowboy prairie-style cooking. At No Place, we place a major emphasis on cooking the way it was done over the open range dating back to pre–Civil War days.

In 1996, I became a partner of the Y.O. Ranch Restaurant in Dallas's West End Historic District. It features my Tex-Mex, wild game, and prairie recipes. In 1997, I added another Tex-Mex restaurant, Matt's in Jefferson, in the wonderful East Texas town of Jefferson, which is on the highway going toward the racetracks and casinos in Shreveport, Louisiana.

Imagine all the hungry bellies that would have been denied their just rewards had Delfino Martinez not eluded the Federales those many years ago.

My Love for Tex-Mex Cooking

Ever since I was a pup, I've eaten Mexican food, but the first time I ever heard someone labeled a Mexican chef, she wasn't even Mexican. She was a nice Anglo at least famous enough to be interviewed for a newspaper article. The story said she was famous, so I guess she must have been.

Up high in the article, she was quoted as saying, "All I do is interior and classical Mexican food. I don't do Tex-Mex."

I was so insulted.

That's when I decided I was not going to do much of anything *but* Tex-Mex. I'm talking Classical Tex-Mex, the way it's been done in the Southwest since the days of the *vaqueros* and real cowboys, whose cast-iron skillets were used and used and used some more.

Perhaps you are aware of the 1990s cooking craze known as Southwestern cuisine? This ain't it.

Southwestern cuisine started out okay and then got too far off into left field. Now, every chef wants to outdo the others. They're all trying to discover some new taste, some new world.

Someday they'll come to grips with the fact that you can't beat the old way. I experiment and do different stuff, but I don't look to do it; it just happens.

It's like going out into the woods. If you go looking for snakes, you know you're going to find some. But sometimes you're out there wandering around and one bites you. That's what I do in the kitchen. I rely on the old ways, but sometimes I stumble onto something that enhances it without insulting it.

Many of the recipes in this book have come to be regarded as basic Tex-Mex, but they are also what the cowboys chowed down on, those many years ago.

Today, Tex-Mex is the fastest-growing ethnic food in America and Europe, particularly in France and England. Tex-Mex is leaps and bounds more popular than the Mexican food of interior Mexico, New Mexico, California, or Arizona.

In Europe, it's a cultural experience, something uniquely American. It's fun food; you can eat most of it with your hands. And you can cook most of it using one skillet, one pot, and one knife.

There are so many flavors and spices in Tex-Mex. . . . I think I'd better hush. My mouth's beginning to water.

Of Skillets, Knives, and Making the Most out of Less

Some people fantasize about riding a white horse and saving damsels in distress. Or they romanticize about being rescued by a tall, dark, handsome stranger.

Maybe I'm crazy, fantasizing about cooking, but I like to cook and I like to think about it all the time. I want to share my love of cooking with you. I am certain that cooking can be rewarding for anyone who really gives it a try. If you can just enjoy a little victory in cooking, something that makes you feel good and think, "Hey, I can do this," you've found an easy way to get people to say nice things about you.

I hope this book makes you many friends. In the process, I encourage you to be like the old gunslinger—that guy who had one gun and one knife. He's the one you had to watch out for. Those old Fancy Dans with a knife in every boot and a slew of guns to pick from were never as good as that guy who practiced with that one pistol and knife.

I use one knife for as many things as possible. I like to cook most everything in one old, black, cast-iron skillet. For my beans, I like to use an earthenware pot. For my soups, I like earthenware pots or porcelain. Stainless steel is also good. I'm not too particularly happy with aluminum, especially for soups or beans.

A good cast-iron skillet retains spices and flavors after each cooking, which is good. You come to love a skillet when it takes on a personality all its own.

A skillet is not supposed to be spick-and-span. The important thing is taking care of it. I never use soap when I'm cleaning out a skillet. Soap goes into the pores and cleans out some of the seasonings and makes a good skillet less stick-resistant.

I always use hot water and scrub the pan real good, and then I put it on the stove and get it very hot and take all the moisture out of it.

Before I put the skillet away, I dry it all over and then I always coat it with oil, usually a vegetable oil.

Another thing: I'm a big believer in serving my food hot. I go to a lot of houses where the hosts throw all the hot food on cold platters and lay 'em out on buffet tables. Then everybody sits around and talks a while, and all I'm thinking is, "The food's getting cold . . . the food's getting cold."

I bring my food out at the last minute, and if I don't have warmers to set them on, I make sure my platters are piping hot.

Oh Lard, How We Love Thee

Because these recipes emphasize how cooking used to be done over a prairie fire, perhaps it's time we bow our heads and pay homage to the lard.

Cowboys used hog lard. I know it's supposed to be nasty stuff health-wise; and so, in these recipes you are encouraged to use the oil of your choice. If you want to season your oil, heat it for a minute and, while continuing to heat, add 4 strips of bacon, half a small sliced onion, and 4 cloves of crushed garlic. As the ingredients brown, pull them out. The seasoned oil will give you the flavor of hog lard without as much cholesterol.

On the other hand, if you've been spending your days at a fitness center and you don't mind an occasional fat binge, here's a good recipe for homemade lard:

Into a large pot containing $2^1/_2$ quarts of water, place 4 pounds of pork fat back, washed and cut in chunks (the size does not matter). After it comes to a boil, add 2 teaspoons of salt. Maintain a low boil over medium heat until the fat is rendered.

Remove the pot from the heat and discard the fat back. Strain the liquid into jars and refrigerate it until you're ready to chow down.

Cook refried beans in this lard, and you may get your first glimpse of heaven.

Cookin' with the One That Brung You

In 1993, I was honored to be the lead speaker for the National Convention of Food Editors at the luxurious Crescent Hotel in Dallas. Afterward, food writers and editors kept coming up and asking, "Where can I find a copy of your cookbook?"

Well, here it is. You will find the recipes basic and easy to follow. You will be surprised, for example, at how easy it is to make the most tender of chicken fried steaks, with gravy that consistently thrills your taste buds.

Dancing with the one that brung us has always been a rule of thumb in Texas. Staying close to what you hold dear, to what makes your little ol' heart pitter-patter, is what this cookbook is all about.

You're not going to see chile ancho sauces with pureed mango or mesquite seed sauces. To a great extent, this is the way it really used to be. And I still dare anybody to beat the old way.

These recipes can be used in the kitchen, on your patio, or while you are camping or hunting or fishing.

When I first began discussing the possibility of doing a cookbook, I was emphatic about one thing: I wanted it to be a real working cookbook. I said, "Please don't make it coffee-table pretty; make it usable."

We have. Enjoy.

1

Breakfast

◆

Huevos Rancheros

On one of those bright summer mornings of my youth, I had a hankering to rush outside and play. As usual, my granny, Maria Gaytan, was shuffling around in the kitchen. I still remember the way the light danced through the kitchen window, over my shoulder and onto Granny's little feet as she pitter-pattered around. "Eat some breakfast before you go," she insisted.

Well, there was a lot of playing that needed to be done, and I was in a hurry to get to it. But when I saw what Granny put in front of me, I thought it looked pretty good. Once I started eating, I was a huevos rancheros fan for life.

I didn't mind staying in the kitchen just a little bit longer.

Makes 4 servings

- 1 batch Ranchero Salsa (page 31)
- 6 tablespoons vegetable oil or other oil of your choice
- 8 corn tortillas
- 1 cup shredded Monterey Jack cheese
- 8 eggs

Make a batch of Ranchero Salsa by following the recipe, but use jalapeño or serrano chile peppers instead of bell peppers.

In a skillet, warm the oil to 350°. Using tongs, dip the tortillas in the oil, only 2 or 3 seconds on each side, and halfway overlap them as you place each tortilla on a baking platter. Spoon 1/2 cup Ranchero Salsa over every 2 tortillas (which is 1 serving). Sprinkle 1/4 cup cheese per 2 tortillas. Heat an oven to 350° and bake the raggedly stacked tortillas, salsa, and cheese for 3 to 4 minutes, until the cheese melts.

In the skillet with the oil, fry the eggs sunny side up or over easy. When the eggs are ready, place 2 cheesy tortillas on each plate, and lay 2 eggs on top.

Serving Suggestions:
- ✛ Serve with beans, rice, or fried potatoes.
- ✛ Serve the left-over salsa on the side, for those desiring more spunk.

REMEMBERING EL RANCHO AND YESTERDAY

Janie Martinez

My son, Matt, started cooking when he was very young. One day my mother, Maria Gaytan, was with him in the kitchen when Matt said he wanted to cook up some scrambled eggs.

I spent my days cooking in the kitchen at El Rancho, and my mother was always at home in the kitchen with Little Matt, making sure he didn't burn himself.

That's where he fell in love with cooking.

Skillet-Style Huevos Rancheros

If you're out in the middle of nowhere, without an oven in sight, do not despair. You can still have huevos rancheros the way the old buckaroos did.

Makes 4 servings

1	batch Ranchero Salsa (page 31)	4	flour tortillas
8	eggs		

In a skillet, make a batch of Ranchero Salsa by following the recipe, but using jalapeño or serrano chile peppers instead of bell peppers.

In a bowl, crack the eggs without breaking the yolks. Carefully spoon the eggs over the salsa in the skillet, trying not to break the yolks. Cover the skillet and fry on low heat for 2 or 3 minutes, until the eggs are to your liking.

Warm the flour tortillas and place one flat on each dinner plate. Take the skillet to the table, and allow your guests to spoon the eggs over the tortillas.

Optional:
- About ¼ cup Monterey Jack cheese per tortilla may be ladled onto the eggs just before serving.

Serving Suggestions:
- Serve with beans, rice, or fried potatoes.
- Serve the left-over salsa on the side, for those desiring more spunk.

Matt Jr. at the age of ten, looking angelic

Embueltos

One day my mom was making an omelette and I couldn't believe she was putting shrimp in it. Ends up she was making embueltos.

Eating eggs at night has never been a big deal to me, but we've sold a whole lot of embueltos at dinnertime at Matt's El Rancho in Austin. Certain people come through the front door with EMBUELTOS written all over their faces. They don't even look at the menu.

I love embueltos in the morning, with some refried beans and tortillas.

I'm telling you, it doesn't get any better than that.

Makes 4 servings

1 batch Ranchero Salsa (page 31)	1/2 cup sour cream
1 pound raw jumbo shrimp (20 count), cleaned and deveined	1/2 cup half and half
8 tablespoons butter or oil of your choice	2 cups shredded Monterey Jack cheese
8 eggs	Fresh flat-leaf parsley or cilantro, as a garnish

In a large skillet, make the batch of Ranchero Salsa, per directions. Cube the shrimp into 1/2-inch-thick pieces, and add to the salsa at very low heat, letting them cook for 4 or 5 minutes. Reserve the shrimp and sauce in a warm pan while making 4 omelettes.

In a second skillet, heat the butter or oil to moderate. For each omelette, use a fork to beat 2 eggs at a time in a bowl, and pour them into the skillet. In another bowl, combine the half and half and sour cream. When the eggs begin to set and are almost firm, place the omelettes on a large baking dish.

Preheat the oven to 375°. On half of each omelette, spoon 1/4 cup of the creamy mixture, then 1/4 cup Monterey Jack cheese, and some of the shrimp with only 1 tablespoon of the salsa. Fold each omelette in half, and place the 4 of them on a baking dish.

Matt Martinez's Culinary Frontier

Pour $1/2$ cup of the salsa over the outside of each omelette. Sprinkle the remaining Monterey Jack over the sauce, and bake for 4 to 5 minutes, until the cheese melts.

Before serving, garnish with the parsley or cilantro.

Optional:

♦ Before baking, I prefer to sprinkle on $1/2$ teaspoon (or, to your taste) grated Parmesan cheese.

Serving Suggestions:

✚ Serve embueltos with your favorite vegetable or crisp salad.
✚ Serve the left-over salsa on the side, for those desiring more spunk.

Scrambled Eggs with Chorizo

Serve these eggs with flour or corn tortillas, with hot sauce on the side so that you can add it to taste after you've had a bite. Although this recipe calls for 2 tablespoons of jalapeño or serrano chile peppers, the brave or hungover are encouraged to double, even triple, the dosage.

Makes 4 to 6 servings

1 pound Simple Chorizo (page 32)	6 eggs
3 tablespoons oil of your choice	1/2 cup chopped tomato
2 tablespoons finely chopped onion	Shredded Monterey Jack or American cheese (optional)
2 tablespoons finely chopped jalapeño or serrano chile pepper	1 teaspoon salt, or to taste

In a 10-inch skillet, combine the chorizo, oil, onion, and peppers. Sauté over moderate heat 4 or 5 minutes, until the pork is cooked and the onion is translucent.

In a bowl, combine the eggs and chopped tomato. Beat lightly.

Add the eggs to the cooked chorizo mixture in the skillet. Scramble the eggs over moderate heat until firm. This should take 1 1/2 to 2 minutes. Sprinkle the cheese, if using it, over the eggs and chorizo just before serving. Salt to taste.

Atole

Whenever I know I'm going to put in a hard day and maybe not eat again for a while, I have atole (ah-TOLL-lay) in the morning. It's guaranteed to bring smiles and sunshine, even on the gloomiest, cloudiest days.

I was sick once as a boy, and my granny told me, "All of the brave Aztec warriors always had a lot of atole before going off to fight."

She said atole was made from corn, and corn came from God. That's why it is such an incredible source of fuel.

It also tastes good with an assortment of toppings. I've even been known to use it as a stress-time drink, with whiskey.

Makes 2 to 3 servings

- 1 (12-ounce) can evaporated milk
- 12 ounces water
- 1/4 cup masa harina
- 1/4 teaspoon vanilla extract
- 1/4 teaspoon ground cinnamon, or to taste
- 2 tablespoons light brown sugar, or to taste

Combine all the ingredients in a saucepan and vigorously whisk the mixture. Place it on your stove over moderate heat without allowing it to come to a boil.

Add more cinnamon or sugar according to taste. And if you're lonely, depressed, perhaps feeling a little suicidal, you may add brandy or whiskey to taste. Serve in preheated cups.

East Pasture Eggs and Rice

When I was in my teens and early twenties, my buddies and I used to hunt on some wooded, rocky, Hill Country property not far from Austin. On the east side of the land was a pasture.

I once joined my friends there late one night after catering a party. I still had my leftovers in the car. We got to drinking saki on past midnight, and we decided to stay over instead of driving back to Austin all sakied up.

It's amazing how the rocks don't bother you when you fall asleep with saki on your brain.

The next day, everybody was hollering for breakfast. I had some soy sauce and rice and eggs and whatnot, so I threw together what we now call East Pasture Eggs and Rice. You do not have to be in a pasture when you eat this, but it has never hurt to have one nearby.

Makes 4 to 6 servings

6 eggs	1/3 cup coarsely chopped celery or bean sprouts
1 cup cooked white rice	1 tablespoon light soy sauce
1/4 cup whole milk	1/4 cup oil of your choice or grease (bacon drippings is best)
1/3 cup coarsely chopped hot peppers or bell peppers	4 drops sesame oil (optional)
1/3 cup coarsely chopped sweet white onion	

Whisk the eggs in a large bowl and add the rice, milk, peppers, onion, celery or sprouts, and soy sauce.

Over a moderate fire, heat the grease and sesame oil in an iron skillet or a nonstick pan. Add the egg mixture and let it set, as you would an omelette, to your liking. I prefer to pull them off when my eggs have set and no longer have runny spots.

Serving Suggestion:
✦ As a hearty late breakfast, serve East Pasture Eggs and Rice with Refried Beans (page 99), Chile con Queso (page 59), flour tortillas, and a cold beer.

Migas

Migas go all the way back to Old Mexico. It's a wonderful dish that emphasizes just how frugal a Mexican kitchen can be. Almost nothing need go to waste. With migas, a tortilla beyond its prime is suddenly a treasure again. It's a prize on any morning plate.

Makes 4 to 6 servings

1/4 cup oil of your choice	1/2 teaspoon black pepper
12 corn tortillas	3/4 teaspoon salt
1/2 cup coarsely chopped onion	1 teaspoon crushed and finely chopped garlic
6 eggs	
1 cup coarsely chopped tomatoes	1 cup shredded Monterey Jack or American cheese
1 large jalapeño or 3 serrano chile peppers, finely chopped	

In a large skillet, heat the oil to 350°. Cut or tear the tortillas into bite-size pieces. Sauté the tortillas until they are crisp. Add the onion and sauté for about 1 minute.

In a bowl, beat the eggs. Add the tomatoes, chile peppers, black pepper, salt, and garlic, and thoroughly beat them into the eggs.

Pour the egg mixture onto the tortillas. Cook the eggs 3 or 4 minutes, until they begin to set, stirring and flipping them in the process. Add the cheese and continue stirring and flipping until the eggs are completely set.

Optional:

♦ For spicier, meatier migas, add 1 cup of your favorite sausage, bacon, chorizo, or chopped ham at the time the onions are added.

Serving Suggestion:

✦ Migas are best served immediately, with Refried Beans (page 99), flour tortillas, and your favorite hot sauce.

One-Eyed Jack

When you're all alone on a queasy morning—a morning made queasy by the night before—follow these instructions:

Crawl out of bed. Go to the kitchen. Make yourself a One-Eyed Jack, with hot sauce and one Lone Star beer.

Return to bed immediately after eating. Within one hour, healing will occur.

Send payment—cash is preferable—to Dr. Matt Martinez, Jr.

Makes 1 serving

1 thick slice of white bread (Texas toast is thickest)	1 egg
2 teaspoons or 2 pats butter	Pinch of grated Parmesan or other grating cheese of your choice

Pinch out a hole in the center of the bread large enough to hold the egg yolk. Immediately eat the pinched bread, which will soon be calming your belly.

With your skillet on medium heat, toast the "holy" bread in the butter. When the toast is browned to your liking, gently break the egg in the center of the toast. Let it cook slightly, until it starts to get firm, then flip it over—egg and toast together—and cook the other side to taste. Sprinkle the cheese on top; it'll begin to melt by the time you get your plate to the table.

Machacado con Huevos (Shredded Beef with Eggs)

Here's an old standby from the heart of Mexico. It was a favorite of the vaqueros who rode the wild and woolly regions of Old Mexico and what is now the southwestern portions of the United States.

Makes 4 to 6 servings

3 tablespoons bacon drippings or vegetable oil	1/2 cup finely chopped jalapeño or serrano chile peppers
1 1/2 pounds dried meat of your choice or beef jerky, shredded	8 eggs
1/2 cup finely chopped white onion	1 teaspoon salt
1 cup finely chopped tomatoes	1/2 teaspoon black pepper

In a skillet, heat the oil on low. Add the machacado (beef) and onion, and sauté for 2 to 3 minutes on low heat. If using jerky, pound out and shred it into pieces first. Add the tomatoes and peppers, and sauté for 2 to 3 minutes. Add the eggs, salt, and pepper, and scramble thoroughly on low heat, until the eggs are firm like an omelette.

Serving Suggestions:
+ Serve as a breakfast entrée with beans, rice, or fried potatoes.
+ Fold the machacado into corn or flour tortillas, to make breakfast tacos.

Breakfast Corncakes

You'll find three corncake recipes in this book, each in a different section. Breakfast Corncakes are to be eaten like pancakes, with your favorite syrup or honey and maybe some bacon or sausage on the side.

Makes a stack of 4 to 6 corncakes

1/4 cup flour	2 tablespoons vegetable shortening
3/4 cup yellow cornmeal	1 egg
1/2 teaspoon baking soda	1 cup buttermilk
2 teaspoons sugar	2 tablespoons vegetable oil
1/4 teaspoon vanilla extract	
1/4 teaspoon ground cinnamon (optional)	

In a mixing bowl, combine all the ingredients except the egg, buttermilk, and oil. Mix thoroughly until the shortening is well distributed. Add the egg and buttermilk, and whisk thoroughly until everything is blended.

Lightly coat a skillet with the vegetable oil and, over medium heat, pour 1/3 to 1/2 cup of batter into the pan. Fry 'em and flip 'em just as you would pancakes, until each cake is golden brown. Stack the cakes and keep them warm while making the rest.

Hard-Time Tacos
(aka No-Meat Potatoes and Eggs)

Even in the hardest of times, you can enjoy a breakfast without the pleasures of meat.

This recipe also makes an excellent filling between slices of white bread for a "home boy" sandwich.

Makes 4 to 6 servings

1 cup oil of your choice (not olive)	1 cup coarsely chopped onions
2 large (approximately 2 pounds total) potatoes, diced or sliced 1/2 inch thick	3–4 jalapeños, quartered
	2 teaspoons Texas Sprinkle (page 42)
6 large eggs	2 cups grated Monterey Jack or American cheese, loosely packed
1/2 cup whole milk	
1 cup coarsely chopped tomatoes	4–6 flour tortillas
1/2 teaspoon salt	

In a large skillet, heat the oil to hot. To test the oil, splash 1 or 2 drops of water into a corner of the skillet; if the oil "spits" back, it's ready.

Add the potatoes to the skillet and fry them until they are golden brown on both sides. With a slotted spoon, remove the potatoes from the oil and drain them on paper towels.

Discard the oil from the skillet.

In a bowl, lightly beat the eggs with the milk, tomatoes, and salt.

Add the onions and jalapeños to the skillet and sauté them for approximately 1 minute. Add the drained potatoes and the Texas Sprinkle, and continue to sauté until the onions are translucent.

Add the egg mixture to the pan and scramble to your taste, roughly 2 to 3 minutes. Add the cheese. Stir once, and serve immediately with flour tortillas and your favorite hot sauce.

Breakfast Tacos

These are similar to Hard-Time Tacos (above), except now you're able to afford the meat. Cowboys, by the way, do not seed their jalapeños. The seeds add more fire.

Makes 4 to 6 servings

- 1 cup oil of your choice (not olive)
- 2 large (approximately 2 pounds total) potatoes, diced or sliced 1/2 inch thick
- 6 large eggs
- 1/2 cup whole milk
- 1/2 teaspoon salt
- 2 cups coarsely chopped cooked meat of your choice (bacon, chorizo, ham, sausage, left-over fajitas, brisket, or shredded meat)

- 1 cup coarsely chopped onions
- 3–4 jalapeños, quartered
- 2 teaspoons Texas Sprinkle (page 42)
- 1 cup grated Monterey Jack or American cheese, loosely packed
- 4–6 flour tortillas

In a large skillet, heat the oil to hot. To test the oil, splash 1 or 2 drops of water into a corner of the skillet; if the oil "spits" back, it's ready.

Add the potatoes and fry until golden brown on both sides. With a slotted spoon, remove the potatoes from the oil and drain on paper towels. Discard the oil from the skillet.

In a bowl, lightly beat the eggs with the milk, salt, and cooked meat.

Add the onions and jalapeños to the skillet and sauté for approximately 1 minute. Add the drained potatoes and the Texas Sprinkle, and continue to sauté 2 to 3 minutes, until the onion is translucent.

Add the egg mixture to the potatoes. Scramble the eggs to your taste: runny, soft, or firm like an omelette. When the eggs are almost done, fold in the cheese.

When the cheese has melted, spoon the filling over flour tortillas and fold them into soft tacos. Add your favorite hot sauce and chow down.

Cactus and Eggs

Scientists and doctors have found that the cactus plant provides amazing benefits to those with diabetes, among other illnesses. Cacti have the kind of internal healing properties that the aloe vera plant does for outer cuts and burns.

Cactus is destined to be a healthy, trend food of the future, though it may be a good deal more than just a trend.

Makes 4 to 6 servings

4 fresh cactus pads (about 2 cups), or 1 (15-ounce) jar sliced cactus	1 teaspoon crushed and finely chopped garlic
3 tablespoons oil (lard or bacon drippings best)	1 jalapeño (leave the seeds if you want your meal hotter), quartered
1 cup coarsely chopped onions	6 eggs, beaten
1 tablespoon chili powder	Salt and black pepper, to taste

If using fresh cacti: Thinly slice the pads and boil them in 2 quarts of salted water until the pads are tender. This will take 30 to 45 minutes. Rinse the cacti in cold water and drain them.

If using a jar of cacti: Open the jar and drain off the water. Rinse each cactus in cold water.

In a skillet, heat the oil to hot and sauté the onions in it. When the onions are translucent—in 2 to 3 minutes—add the cacti, chili powder, garlic, and jalapeño. Sauté the ingredients for 1 to 2 minutes. Add the eggs, and scramble over medium heat until the eggs are set. Season with the salt and pepper.

Optional:

◆ If cactus cannot be found, a can of french-cut green beans may be used.

Serving Suggestion:

✦ Serve Cactus and Eggs immediately, with Refried Beans (page 99) and flour or corn tortillas.

II

Toppings:
Sauces,
Gravies,
Broths, Picos

Matt's Smoked Salsa

I believe the salsa we serve at Matt's Rancho Martinez in Dallas is unique, and as tasty as any you will find. We try to make it a little runny, but with still enough texture to lop some on a tortilla chip. Actually, this smoked salsa is a welcome addition to almost any kind of Tex-Mex dish requiring a bit of spunk.

If you don't have a smoker, you can use a barbecue pit. Sorry, but an oven won't do.

Makes 4 to 6 servings

3	whole medium tomatoes	2	teaspoons vegetable oil
1	clove garlic	3	fresh jalapeños or 6 serrano chile peppers
1/2	medium sweet white onion		
3/4	teaspoon salt	1/2	cup water
1	teaspoon distilled white vinegar		

Combine all the ingredients in a heavy pot and place the pot (no lid) in a smoker for 1 1/2 to 2 hours, until the vegetables are soft. Do not allow the sauce to become dry; add more water if needed. Mash (do not blend) the vegetables in the pot. Adjust the salt to taste.

Keeps 2 weeks in the refrigerator in an air-tight container.

Optional:

♦ For a thicker salsa, combine 1 tablespoon cornstarch with 2 tablespoons water. While the sauce is still hot, drizzle the extra ingredients into the salsa. Simmer it on low heat for 5 to 10 minutes, until you acquire the desired thickness. Simply add a bit more water if the salsa becomes too chunky.

Tomatillo Salsa (Green Sauce)

Tomatillo salsa, also known as salsa verde, goes well with chicken enchiladas, flautas, quesadillas, and much, much more. Actually, it's best wherever you like it, you being the judge of your own taste buds.

Makes 6 to 8 servings

- 3 tablespoons oil of your choice
- 1 cup finely chopped onions
- 1 pound tomatillos (little green tomatoes), finely chopped
- 1 tablespoon finely chopped jalapeño or serrano chile pepper
- 1 tablespoon crushed and finely chopped garlic
- 1/4 cup finely chopped fresh cilantro, loosely packed
- 3 cups Chicken Broth (canned, or see page 47)
- 1 tablespoon cornstarch
- 1 teaspoon sugar

Heat the oil in a heavy saucepot and brown the onions. Mix in the tomatillos, chile peppers, garlic, and cilantro. Add 2½ cups of the broth, and simmer on low heat for about 10 minutes. Drizzle in the cornstarch, sugar, and the last ½ cup of broth, and simmer for 2 to 3 minutes on low heat while the salsa thickens.

If the sauce is too thick, add a little more broth to taste, just so it's not runny. Keeps 2 weeks in the refrigerator in an air-tight container.

Ranchero Salsa (Red Sauce)

Those who prefer their salsa hot are encouraged to substitute jalapeños for the bell pepper in this simple, tasty recipe. The celery is what gives the sauce its special sweetness.

Use Ranchero Salsa on enchiladas, Huevos Rancheros (page 11), Chicken-Fried Steak Tampiquena (page 154), Chile Rellenos (page 157), Tostados Compuestas (page 123), and anything else you darn well please.

Makes 4 to 6 servings

2	tablespoons vegetable or olive oil	1 1/2	teaspoons salt
1	cup finely chopped white onions	1/4	teaspoon black pepper
1/2	cup finely chopped celery	1	tablespoon cornstarch
1/2	cup finely chopped green bell pepper	1	(14 1/2-ounce) can whole tomatoes, broken up
1	teaspoon ground cumin	2	cups Chicken or Beef Broth (canned, or see pages 47 and 48)
1/2	teaspoon dried oregano		
1	teaspoon granulated garlic		

Using a thick, heavy saucepot, heat the oil and brown the onions, celery, and bell pepper, for 2 to 3 minutes. Add the remaining ingredients and simmer for 20 minutes on low heat. Use immediately, while the sauce is hot, or refrigerate for later.

Keeps 2 weeks in the refrigerator in an air-tight container.

Simple Chorizo

This chorizo can be used as a flavoring agent for beans, potatoes, eggs, migas, dips, and—for that matter—most anything else that suits your fancy. Such as, the Scrambled Eggs with Chorizo (page 16).

Makes 1 batch

1 pound ground pork	1/2 teaspoon dried oregano
1 teaspoon salt	1/4 teaspoon black pepper
1/2 teaspoon granulated garlic	3 tablespoons chili powder
2 teaspoons ground cumin	1 tablespoon distilled white vinegar

In a bowl, mix all the ingredients together and refrigerate overnight. Or, if preparing for a meal down the road, freeze it.

Seafood Red Sauce

This red sauce is traditional with shrimp cocktail, but it's also great on fried foods. For many, it's basic catfish-eatin' sauce.

Makes 6 to 8 servings

1   (14-ounce) bottle ketchup

2   tablespoons prepared horseradish

2   tablespoons Worcestershire sauce

    Juice of 1 fresh lemon

1   teaspoon prepared French's mustard

    Tabasco sauce, to taste

In a bowl, mix all the ingredients well. Refrigerate the sauce until you're ready to chow down.

Tartar Sauce

Traditional tartar sauce has a way of making fried shrimp and catfish go down smoother.

Makes 6 to 8 servings

1 cup finely chopped onions	2 cups mayonnaise
1 cup finely chopped dill pickles	Juice of 1 fresh lemon

Mix all the ingredients well. Refrigerate, until it's time to roll up your sleeves. It's best to discard the leftovers.

Cilantro Vinaigrette

My favorite variation is a combination of anchovies and blue cheese. It's great on salads (especially spinach), cucumbers and onions, roasted chicken, and beefsteak tomatoes.

Makes 4 to 6 servings

1/4 cup chopped fresh cilantro, loosely packed	1 tablespoon crushed and finely chopped garlic
1/4 cup olive oil	1 teaspoon sugar
1/4 cup canola oil	1/2 teaspoon salt
1/4 cup red wine vinegar	

Put all the ingredients into a blender. Run it on low for 30 seconds. Refrigerate; this vinaigrette keeps indefinitely. Shake vigorously before using.

Optional:

◆ For character, blend in 4 anchovy fillets and one teaspoon of anchovy oil.

◆ For a creamier consistency, add 1/4 cup crumbled blue cheese or Monterey Jack cheese before blending.

Triple-X Garlic Vinaigrette

This is in a dead heat with the Cilantro Vinaigrette (above) as my favorite summer salad dressing. I eat it with everything—it's even good on baked potatoes.

Makes 6 to 8 servings

1 tablespoon crushed and finely chopped fresh garlic (I use 2 tablespoons, but start with this)	2 heaping teaspoons finely chopped green onion (white part only)
1/4 cup olive oil	1 fresh summer tomato, peeled, seeded, and coarsely chopped
1/4 cup canola oil	1 pinch or 1/4 teaspoon sugar
1/4 cup rice vinegar	1/2 teaspoon salt, or to taste

In a bowl, combine all the ingredients. Vigorously whisk them before serving, or put them in a blender on low for 30 seconds. This keeps in the refrigerator for a week to 10 days. Always shake vigorously before using.

Serving Suggestions:

✦ Pour the vinaigrette over sliced cucumbers, raw vegetables, baked or boiled potatoes, or beefsteak tomatoes.

✦ Toss it with cold pasta.

Buttermilk Dressing

I'm a sucker for a sandwich of sliced avocado and cucumber on dark bread, with plenty of crumbled bacon, and Buttermilk Dressing spilling over the sides.

Use also on meaty sandwiches, as a dressing for coleslaws, or as a salad dressing.

Makes 6 to 8 servings

3   slices of bacon

1/2   cup mayonnaise

1/2   cup sour cream

1   cup buttermilk

2   tablespoons finely chopped white onion

1   teaspoon finely chopped fresh cilantro or flat-leaf parsley

1   clove garlic, crushed and finely chopped

1   medium-to-large tomato, peeled, seeded, and finely chopped

Fry the bacon in a skillet until crisp. Remove the bacon from the pan and dab off the excess grease with paper towels, then crumble the bacon up and save it to use as a garnish.

Combine all the remaining ingredients in a bowl. Sprinkle on enough crushed bacon to suit your fancy.

Keeps a week to 10 days in the refrigerator in an air-tight container.

Matt's Simple Barbecue Sauce

Why make it difficult when easy can be really good?

Makes 3 cups, enough for a large brisket

1	lemon	2	tablespoons brown sugar
2	cups ketchup	2	tablespoons distilled white vinegar
2	tablespoons Worcestershire sauce	3	tablespoons orange marmalade
1	teaspoon prepared yellow mustard	2	tablespoons butter (optional)

In a saucepot, thoroughly combine all the ingredients except the butter and bring them to a boil. Reduce the heat and let the sauce simmer for 5 minutes. Stir in the butter, if desired. Use the sauce to baste meat while barbecuing. Also, serve it warm on the side.

This keeps a week to 10 days in the refrigerator in an air-tight container.

Horseradish Sauce

If you're looking for more bang, use this horseradish sauce instead of, or along with, the Simple Barbecue Sauce. Try it with brisket. It makes enough for 4 meaty sandwiches.

Makes about 1/2 cup

- 2 tablespoons prepared white horseradish
- 1/4 cup mayonnaise
- 1/4 cup sour cream

- Juice of 1/2 fresh lemon
- 1/2 teaspoon sugar

In a small bowl, thoroughly mix the ingredients. Chill the sauce and serve it cold. It keeps a week to 10 days in the refrigerator in an air-tight container.

Matt's Dry Rub

I concocted this rub for brisket, chicken, and ribs. For brisket, rub two thirds of the mixture on the fat side and the other third on the bottom before grilling. For chicken or ribs, simply rub on while grilling.

Makes enough for 4 to 5 pounds of meat

1/2 teaspoon ground cumin	1/2 teaspoon chili powder
1/2 teaspoon granulated garlic	1/2 teaspoon cornstarch
1 1/2 teaspoons salt	1/4 teaspoon black pepper

In a small bowl, combine all the ingredients. Apply the rub when it's at room temperature. This keeps indefinitely in the refrigerator.

Black Magic Finishing Sauce

Many of my recipes will call for this finishing sauce, which is a secret recipe (until now) that has been in the Martinez family for years. It is a natural flavor enhancer for beef, poultry, fish, all seafood, wild game, and vegetables.

Use approximately 1 teaspoon of finishing sauce per 3 ounces of meat or vegetable, roughly $2^1/_2$ to 3 teaspoons for an 8-ounce steak.

Makes enough for six 8-ounce steaks

$^1/_4$ cup light soy sauce	1 tablespoon red wine vinegar
1 tablespoon red wine	

In a small bowl, combine all the ingredients.

Dab on the finishing sauce just before taking the meat or vegetables off the fire; it'll only be on the fire a few seconds.

There's no need to freeze or refrigerate this finishing sauce. It keeps indefinitely in a covered container at room temperature.

Texas Sprinkle

You might say my dad began his restaurant career at the age of 6. Remember his dad, Delfino? He was the one who almost got hanged before the family tree extended as far as my limbs.

When Dad's parents moved to Austin, they began selling tamales and pralines from a wooden cart on Congress Avenue and all around the Capitol building. My dad was 6 years old and right there with them. That was back in the 1920s.

At times, they had to go as far away as San Antonio to buy certain ingredients. They made the 2-to-3-day ride together in a little red wagon pulled by a horse named Nellie. Dad has always talked about that horse like it was a member of the family. Nellie must have looked quite stoic and proud, through my dad's little-boy eyes, as she clopped along, pulling them all those miles, never needing a tune-up.

On one of those journeys to San Antonio, they stopped near Buda, Texas, and baptized my dad in a baptismal trough that had been built on the property.

Today, the packaging company for Jardine Foods is located on the land of Dad's baptism, and Jardine Foods was the first to distribute my Texas Sprinkle and Black Magic Finishing Sauce.

Now you know why I believe this sprinkle is holy water.

By the way, the cracker meal takes the bite from the garlic and pepper, and makes it real forgiving if you use too much of either.

Makes 12 to 15 servings

4	tablespoons granulated garlic	1/2	teaspoon dried thyme
2	tablespoons salt	1	teaspoon white pepper
1	tablespoon black pepper	7	teaspoons cracker meal

Shake the ingredients in a jar. It's best to wait until the next day before using the mixture, thus allowing the spices to be absorbed into the cracker meal.

Keep Texas Sprinkle in an air-tight container out of direct sunlight. There's no need to freeze or refrigerate it. I've kept it for up to 2 years.

Perfect Cream Gravy

Talk about religious experiences, cream gravy has long been a spiritually uplifting gift from the food gods. Unfortunately, too many people have a hard time making gravy turn out just right on a consistent basis. Here's how.

Makes 6 to 8 servings

- 6 tablespoons drippings from frying steaks
- 6 tablespoons flour

- 3 cups warm whole milk
- Salt and black pepper, to taste

Drain all but 6 tablespoons of fat from the pan in which the steaks are fried. Add the flour, and stir it over medium heat 3 to 4 minutes, until lightly browned.

Add the warmed milk and stir, scraping and loosening any brown bits from the pan, until the gravy enjoys a thick consistency. This will only take a minute or two.

Season the gravy with salt and pepper and serve it with the steaks.

Matt's Lighter Gravy

Pour this over chicken-fried steaks and chicken-fried chicken, or dip plain ol' tasty fried chicken into it.

Makes 6 to 8 servings

2 tablespoons butter	2 cups Chicken Broth (canned, or see page 47)
1/2 cup sliced mushrooms	1 cup milk
1/2 cup finely chopped onion	Salt and black pepper, to taste
3 tablespoons cornstarch	

Drain the fat from the pan in which the steaks cooked, but leave the brown bits on the bottom. Add the butter, mushrooms, and onion, and cook over medium heat, stirring, until lightly browned. This will take 2 to 3 minutes. Thoroughly mix in the cornstarch. Add the broth and milk. Continue cooking over medium heat, stirring and scraping up the bits from the bottom of the pan, until the gravy has thickened. This should take a minute or 2.

Season the gravy with salt and pepper. Before serving the gravy with the steaks, simmer it for 2 to 3 minutes at a very low heat.

Summer Pico

This pico is meant to celebrate summer tomatoes at their peak without overpowering them. Serve it with tacos, steaks, chicken, fish, and fajitas. Summer Pico is also an excellent guacamole garnish.

Makes 4 to 6 servings

- 2 cups freshly chopped tomatoes (1/4-inch cubes), peeled and seeded if desired
- 1 tablespoon finely chopped fresh jalapeño or serrano chile pepper
- 1 tablespoon finely chopped fresh cilantro, loosely packed
- 1 tablespoon finely chopped white onion
- 1 clove garlic, crushed and finely chopped
- 2 tablespoons vegetable oil
- 1 tablespoon fresh lemon juice

  Salt, to taste

In a bowl, mix all the ingredients well. Pico is best served immediately. It can be refrigerated for a day, but no longer, in a sealed container.

Pico de Gallo

Use this pico on the same dishes as the Summer Pico above. Garlic lovers, please feel free to spice things up with 1 teaspoon or more fresh garlic, crushed and finely chopped.

Makes 4 to 6 servings

- 1 cup freshly chopped tomatoes (1/4-inch cubes), peeled and seeded if desired

- 1/4 cup finely chopped sweet white onion

- 1/4 cup finely chopped jalapeño or serrano chile pepper

- 1/4 cup finely chopped fresh cilantro, loosely packed

- 2 tablespoons olive or vegetable oil

- 1 tablespoon red wine vinegar or fresh lemon juice

  Salt, to taste

In a bowl, mix all the ingredients well. Pico is best served immediately. It can be refrigerated for a day, but no longer, in a sealed container.

Chicken (or Turkey) Broth

I'm giving you 2 recipes for accent broths, which are not meant to be spicy or too strong. They complement soups, pastas, beans, and sauces. The broth is best refrigerated overnight.

Makes 4 to 5 cups

- 2 pounds chicken or turkey parts (neck, back, wings, giblets, but no livers, please)

- 1 cup coarsely chopped peeled carrots

- 1 cup coarsely chopped sweet white onions

- 1 cup coarsely chopped celery (with a few chopped leaves)

   Juice of 1/2 fresh lemon

- 2 1/2 quarts water

- 2 teaspoons salt

In a 4-quart soup pot, combine all the ingredients and bring them to a boil. Simmer the broth uncovered on low heat for 3 hours, occasionally skimming the top. Strain to remove all the solids.

Store the broth in 1-cup air-tight containers or plastic storage bags. Refrigerate the broth overnight. The next day, again skim off as much fat as possible.

Always freeze or refrigerate the unused broth.

Keeps 3 to 4 days if refrigerated; 3 to 4 months in the freezer.

Beef Broth

As with the Chicken Broth, above, this Beef Broth is used to accent soups, pastas, beans, and sauces. It is not meant to be overpowering or strong. Make it as you would the Chicken Broth above but use 2 pounds beef bones (with meat and marrow, if possible) instead of the chicken parts.

Chipotle Sauce
(The Basics, for Adult Parties)

In olden Mexico, they used to come out of the mountains to pick the ripe chipotle peppers at the end of the season. They would smoke the peppers over mesquite, giving the sauce just a whisper of the good, sweet smoke. They kept their fires airy, so the peppers would burn clean.

For those who prefer spicy chicken, this makes enough sauce for 4 fryers, or makes a good wet rub for 8 pounds of ribs. It's also good for hot dogs, Fried Catfish (page 198), and chicken wings.

You braver souls feel free to use your leftover sauce on the side.

Makes 7 ounces

1 (7-ounce) can chipotle peppers	1/2 cup coarsely chopped onion
1 tablespoon Worcestershire sauce	2 tablespoons distilled white vinegar
1 teaspoon crushed and finely chopped garlic	1 teaspoon salt

Put all the ingredients into a blender and blend them for 30 seconds on low.

The sauce is now ready to spice up: Per your taste, use ketchup, mustard, barbecue sauce, mayonnaise, or ranch dressing. For each 1/2 cup of your preferred condiment, add 1 tablespoon of Chipotle Sauce.

This keeps for several weeks in the refrigerator in an air-tight container.

Poor-Boy Enchilada Sauce

This is one of the original South Texas sauces. Cowboys really flipped over it back in the days before folks made a habit of putting meat and other fillings in enchiladas.

Makes 6 to 8 servings

1/4 cup lard, vegetable shortening, or vegetable oil

1/4 cup flour

1/2 teaspoon black pepper

1 teaspoon salt

1 1/2 teaspoons granulated garlic

2 teaspoons ground cumin

1/2 teaspoon dried oregano

2 tablespoons chili powder

3 cups water or Chicken Broth (canned, or see page 47)

In a large skillet, heat the lard to medium hot. Stir in the flour and continue stirring until it turns a very light brown. This will take about 3 to 4 minutes.

Add all of the dry ingredients and continue to cook for 1 minute, constantly stirring and blending the ingredients. Add the water or broth, mixing and stirring until the sauce thickens, approximately 1 1/2 to 2 minutes.

Turn the heat to low and let the sauce simmer for 15 to 20 minutes. Add more water to adjust the thickness to your preference.

Pour the sauce over the enchiladas of your choice.

This keeps a week to 10 days in the refrigerator in an air-tight container; it also keeps well in the freezer.

III

Starters:
Appetizers,
Soups,
Salads

Stuffed Jalapeños

Our chile rellenos and stuffed jalapeños have been the two signature dishes of my family's Austin restaurant for almost a half-century.

My mother was the first person I ever saw make a stuffed jalapeño. Once we started making them at Matt's El Rancho, everybody else in Austin tried to do the same thing. Much to their dismay, their cheese kept floating to the top as the jalapeños fried. Try as they might, other cooks could not figure out what they were doing wrong.

What nobody realized was that my mother was freezing her stuffed jalapeños, getting them rock-hard before dropping them into the fryer. By the time the jalapeños got crisp and golden and crunchy on the outside, the inside would be melted and filled with spicy, cheesy flavors.

My mother also uses basically the same battering technique on stuffed peppers that we use for chicken, chicken-fried steaks, and fried vegetables. It's simple: She dusts them in flour seasoned with a little salt and pepper, dunks them in buttermilk, then dusts them back in the flour.

Steer clear of buying jalapeños that are wrinkled. They begin to lose their flavor and texture by then. Always try to cook with jalapeños while they are still shiny green and tight-skinned.

Makes 4 to 6 servings (12 stuffed jalapeños)

12	whole pickled jalapeños	2	cups buttermilk
2	cups grated Monterey Jack or American cheese	2	cups cracker meal or seasoned bread crumbs
1	cup flour		Oil of your choice, for deep-frying

Slit open one side of each jalapeño and discard all the seeds and membranes. Rinse the jalapeños in cold water.

Stuff the jalapeños with the cheese, roll them in the flour, dunk them in the buttermilk, then roll them in the cracker meal.

Place the stuffed jalapeños in the freezer for 2 to 3 hours, until they are completely frozen.

Using enough oil to give you about an inch in depth, fry the peppers to a golden brown at 375°. The entire batch should be ready in 3 to 4 minutes. The quicker you eat 'em after frying, the better they are.

REMEMBERING EL RANCHO AND YESTERDAY

Mike Jones

As a sportswriter for the Dallas Morning News *(1968–80) and* Fort Worth Star-Telegram *(1982–current), Mike has made many a social call to Austin, covering almost every facet of collegiate sports. Those trips still include an El Rancho stop or two.*

Sometimes, I get these cravings for the stuffed jalapeños. Once, while covering the Texas Relays track and field championships, I ate every meal [at El Rancho] for three days. Five meals in a row, twice a day for two days, and once on get-away day.

I stopped for one reason. The track meet ended.

Salmon-Stuffed Jalapeños

See the Buttermilk Dressing recipe (page 37). It goes well with salmon and makes a great dipping sauce for these stuffed jalapeños.

Makes 4 to 6 servings (12 stuffed jalapeños)

1 (14-ounce) can pink salmon	12 whole pickled jalapeños
4 tablespoons minced onion	1 cup flour
1/4 tablespoon black pepper	2 cups buttermilk
1/2 cup milk	2 cups cracker meal or seasoned bread crumbs
1 egg, beaten	
2 tablespoons freshly grated Parmesan cheese	Oil of your choice, for deep-frying

In a large bowl, thoroughly mix the salmon, onion, black pepper, milk, egg, and cheese.

Slit open one side of each jalapeño and discard all the seeds and membranes. Rinse the jalapeños in cold water (only the foolish would rub their eyes from this point on). Stuff the jalapeños with the salmon mixture.

Roll the jalapeños in the flour, dunk them in the buttermilk, then roll them in the cracker meal.

Using enough oil to give you about an inch in depth, heat the oil to 370°. Fry the stuffed jalapeños to a golden brown, about 3 to 4 minutes. Then eat 'em all up.

REMEMBERING EL RANCHO AND YESTERDAY

Denne Freeman

Denne has been Southwest Regional Sports Editor of the Associated Press for thirty years.

In 1968, I had just become sports editor, working out of the Dallas bureau, when I had to fly to Austin to cover a University of Texas football game.

Jones Ramsey was there to meet me as I got off the plane, and he drove directly to El Rancho. I'd never met Jones before, and I'd never heard of El Rancho.

When we arrived, first thing I noticed was the waiting line, snaking into the parking lot. Jones led me right to the front door, with all these people burning holes in the backs of our necks.

We were welcomed inside and immediately seated at the Jones Ramsey Table. We weren't even given a menu. In five minutes, out comes these appetizers—chips, hot sauce, chile con queso, stuffed jalapeños, chile rellenos with raisins and sour cream.

That was for openers.

Then the Jones Ramsey Specials came flying out of the kitchen.

At one point, Jones said, "You know, if I'm ever sentenced to the electric chair and I'm allowed one last meal, I'm gonna come here and order everything on the menu."

I said, "I thought you just did."

The next afternoon, my assignment was to cover a football game at Memorial Stadium on the University of Texas campus. I arrived at the pressbox early, put my typewriter at the Associated Press's designated seat, and headed for the pressbox lunch area.

Lo and behold, there was the Martinez family and all those El Rancho people I'd met the night before, lopping food onto paper plates. Turns out, Ramsey was using El Rancho to cater Texas's home games.

Ramsey loved El Rancho so much, he once told me he had eaten 112 consecutive meals there.

REMEMBERING EL RANCHO AND YESTERDAY

Mike Jones

Before the game, anybody found walking around the Memorial Stadium pressbox with the meal-ticket stub still attached to their press credentials was invariably asked, "You using that?"

Some writers would go back for seconds right away; or, they'd wait until halftime and go eat again.

When the game was over and we were all writing our game stories, Ramsey would come by and hand out some of Matt's homemade cookies.

That was our reward for making it through the day.

Chile con Queso

As far as I'm concerned, Jones Ramsey was the greatest Sports Information Director in the history of college athletics, and also the one with the happiest belly.

I'm only slightly prejudiced, since Jones spent half his time at my family's Austin restaurant. He may have eaten there more often than I did.

Jones says, "When I was living in Austin and eating at El Rancho regularly, I loved the chile con queso so much, I put it all over everything."

Now you can, too.

Makes 6 to 8 servings

1 tablespoon oil of your choice	1/2 teaspoon salt
1/2 cup finely chopped sweet white onion	2 tablespoons cornstarch
1/2 cup finely chopped bell pepper or jalapeño (or a combination)	1 cup water or Chicken Broth (canned, or see page 47)
1 teaspoon ground cumin	8 ounces shredded cheese (Kraft American is best)
1 teaspoon granulated garlic	1 cup chopped tomatoes

Using a thick, heavy pot, heat the oil and sauté the onion and the dry ingredients for 2 to 3 minutes, until the onion is translucent.

Add the water or broth, and heat 3 to 4 minutes, allowing the sauce to thicken, then add the shredded cheese and tomatoes.

Carefully simmer the queso on low heat for 3 to 5 minutes, adjusting its thickness to suit your taste by adding water or cheese. Serve hot.

REMEMBERING EL RANCHO AND YESTERDAY

Jones Ramsey

Jones was the legendary Sports Information Director at the University of Texas from 1961 to 1983. Retired and living in Ponca City, Oklahoma, Jones confesses that his belly yearns, perhaps even burns, for a good Tex-Mex fix.

I arrived in Austin in 1961 and heard about El Rancho a year later. I'd never heard of Tex-Mex food.

I loved the place. I started taking the out-of-town sportswriters there, and pretty soon it was the only place any sportswriter in the country wanted to go.

Braniff Airlines had a perfect flight schedule for a lot of the frequent out-of-town writers, and they started planning their arrivals into Austin for eleven-thirty, a quarter to noon, and off we'd go, straight to El Rancho, even before they checked into a hotel.

My favorite waiter was a great guy named Albert. He put six children through college off the money he made at El Rancho. Albert would see me coming and duck in the back and put in the order. He already knew what I wanted.

When the out-of-town writers went to El Rancho by themselves, they'd say, "We want what Jones Ramsey eats." But if Albert wasn't there, nobody knew what they were talking about.

That's because there was no Jones Ramsey Special on the menu.

But Albert knew it consisted of burritos, flour tortillas, beans, and rice, all of it smothered in chile con queso. A lot of folks had it.

I no longer eat traditional Mexican food. My friends in Oklahoma are always bragging about some new Mexican food place worth trying. They take me there, and I leave the food on the plate. I want El Rancho.

Traditional Guacamole

It's difficult for a guacamole recipe to be consistent because avocados vary so much in size, shape, and meatiness.

I prefer to prepare a basic guacamole, then add onion, cilantro, and other ingredients depending on the size of the avocados. Some people want their guacamole spicier, some more garlicky, some with cilantro.

Tomatoes, by the way, give guacamole a good sweetness, and the combination is very complementary.

Makes 2 servings per avocado

Avocados		Salt, to taste
1	teaspoon fresh squeezed lime or lemon juice per avocado	

Cut the avocado in half. Discard the pit, and scoop out the avocado flesh. Discard the skin. Mash the lime juice into the avocado and continue mashing. For the best texture, leave it chunky. Adjust the salt to taste.

Optional:

◆ According to your taste, experiment with adding any or all of the following ingredients by stirring them into the mashed avocado:

1 tablespoon finely chopped sweet white onion

1 tablespoon finely chopped fresh cilantro

1 tablespoon finely chopped fresh jalapeño

1 tablespoon crushed and finely chopped garlic

1 tablespoon tomato, peeled, seeded, and finely chopped

Chorizo Bean Dip

This serves as a nice side dish for grilled chicken or beef. If you use black beans instead of refried beans, use Monterey Jack or farmer's cheese instead of American.

Makes 4 to 6 servings

- 1 tablespoon oil of your choice
- 1/2 pound Simple Chorizo (page 32)
- 1/4 cup finely chopped onion
- 1/4 cup finely chopped jalapeño or serrano chile peppers

- 2 cups Refried Beans (page 99) or cooked black beans (canned is okay)
- 1 cup grated American cheese (or see headnote)

Heat the oil in a skillet and sauté the chorizo, onion, and chile peppers for 4 1/2 to 5 minutes, until the pork is cooked through. Thoroughly mix in the refried or cooked black beans. Heat the oven to 375°.

Place the dip in a baking dish or on a small oven-proof platter. Sprinkle the cheese on top, and bake the dip 4 to 5 minutes, until the cheese melts. Serve it with tortillas or chips.

Queso Flameado (Flaming Cheese)

It's hard to beat this dip for serving with chips or soft tortillas. Eggs go well, too.

Makes 4 to 6 servings

1 tablespoon oil of your choice	1 cup coarsely chopped fresh tomatoes
1 pound Simple Chorizo (page 32)	1 cup shredded Monterey Jack cheese
1/2 cup finely chopped onion	
1/2 cup finely chopped jalapeño or serrano chile peppers	

Heat the oil in a skillet and sauté the chorizo, onion, and chile peppers for 4 1/2 to 5 minutes, until the pork is cooked through. Heat the oven to 375°. Place the sautéed ingredients in an oven-proof dish. Cover them with the tomatoes and cheese, and bake 4 to 5 minutes, until the cheese not only melts but is bubbly hot.

Traditional Nachos

Combinations for nachos are endless. It's best to keep them simple in the beginning. Use your favorite cheeses and beans, and advance to a fancier, more complex mixture as your taste demands.

But remember, go lightly so you will enjoy the taste and texture of the fried chip, which should not be overwhelmed.

Makes enough topping for about 4 tortillas per person

> Fried Corn Tortillas, quartered or halved (page 85)
>
> 1/2 teaspoon beans per tortilla half
>
> Sprinkle of grated cheese of your choice

> 2 cups cooked shredded meat or crumbled taco meat (page 139)
>
> 2 cups vegetables (combination of white onions, jalapeños, and tomatoes)

Cover the bottom of a cookie sheet or platter with the fried tortilla halves. Place the cheese and other toppings of your choice on the tortillas (stack the tortillas on top of each other if you like). Do not overload the tortillas, but adequately cover the chips.

Place the cookie sheet in a 450° oven, or under the broiler, and bake or broil the nachos for 2 to 3 minutes, only until the cheese melts.

Ballpark Nachos

Because of their name and reputation, the following nachos should be eaten outdoors around lots of people. They must be eaten with fingers only. Napkins may be used. Shirtsleeves are best.

Makes about 4 tortillas per person

1 recipe Chile con Queso (page 59)	1 cup sliced pickled jalapeños
2 cups cooked ground meat or shredded meat of your choice	1 cup sliced fresh onion rings
Fried Corn Tortillas, quartered or halved (page 85)	1 cup chopped tomatoes

If you're planning a nacho party, prepare your queso and meat, and keep them warm in the oven. Set out the other assorted toppings.

Have your guests arrange a pile of fried tortilla chips on a 6- to 8-inch plate. Let them sprinkle on the assorted goodies. Then ladle the creamy queso over the chips and toppings.

Tortilla Soup

Most tortilla soups in restaurants are cooked with the tortillas in the soup, and they also throw in cumin and other unnecessary stuff.

This is a light starter soup, good in the winter or summer. Many of the flavors are kept fresh because you don't let the tortillas get soggy in the cooking process; and, you don't put in the tomato, avocado, and cheese while cooking.

Makes 4 servings

1 quart Chicken Broth (canned, or see page 47)	1 serrano chile pepper, finely chopped
8–10 ounces chicken breast, skinned and boned	4 heaping teaspoons grated Monterey Jack cheese
1 medium tomato, finely chopped	1 cup vegetable oil
1 avocado, cubed	4 corn tortillas
1 tablespoon finely chopped fresh cilantro, loosely packed	

In a pan, bring the broth to a boil, then poach the chicken breast uncovered in the broth for 30 minutes over low heat. Remove the chicken and julienne it before putting it back into the broth.

On the side, mix the tomato, avocado, cilantro, chile pepper, and cheese.

In a skillet, heat the oil to 350°. Roll up the corn tortillas into small flutes. Cut the rolled up tortillas crosswise into long, thin strips.

Fry the tortilla strips in the oil for 3 to 4 minutes, until they are crisp. Remove them and drain on paper towels.

Place equal amounts of fried tortillas into each of 4 bowls, and get the bowls hot in an 180° oven for 5 to 10 minutes. Spoon equal amounts (about 1 heaping teaspoon each) mixed vegetables and cheese over the chips. Ladle the hot broth and chicken on top. Serve immediately.

Ceviche

This is a tasty appetizer best served with chips and sliced avocados on the side. Ceviche can also be used as a dressing for salads.

Makes 8 to 10 servings

4 limes, sliced	1 heaping tablespoon crushed garlic
1 lemon, sliced	1 onion, very coarsely chopped
1/2 cup fresh lemon juice	1 bell pepper, seeded and quartered
1/2 cup red wine vinegar	3 jalapeños, finely chopped or sliced
2 teaspoons brown sugar	2 1/2–3 pounds fish (any white-fleshed or mild fish will work, such as striper or white sand bass)
1 cup virgin olive oil	
1 teaspoon black cracked pepper	
2 teaspoons salt	

Mix all the ingredients except the fish in a bowl. Pour the mixture into an air-tight plastic storage bag.

Cut the fish into 1/4-inch strips and thoroughly blend the fish strips with the mixture in the storage bag. Press the air from the bag, and seal the bag.

Pack the storage bag in ice for a minimum of 1 hour but no more than 2; or, refrigerate for 2 to 3 hours. Serve the ceviche cold.

Matt Martinez's Culinary Frontier

Fryer Soup

Chicken or turkey parts may be used in this soup. Never use liver in soup, unless your goal is to chase off unwanted guests.

Makes 4 to 6 servings

1	(2–2 1/2 pounds) fryer	1	heaping teaspoon chopped garlic
3	quarts water	1	cup coarsely chopped zucchini
2	teaspoons salt	1	cup coarsely chopped yellow squash
2	cups coarsely chopped white onions	1	cup corn kernels
1	cup coarsely chopped celery	1/2	cup uncooked white rice
1	cup coarsely chopped carrots		

Wash the fryer in cold water, and cut it into large pieces. Place the fryer pieces in a large pot with the water and salt. Once the water begins to boil on high, reduce the heat to a simmer.

Skim the water and remove all of the floating excess. After 1 hour, remove the fryer. Discard the skin and bones, and reserve the chicken meat. Again, skim the floating fat from the soup.

Add the vegetables to the pot. Simmer for 1 hour.

Return the chicken to the pot, and add the rice. Let the ingredients in the pot simmer uncovered for another 30 minutes, then immediately serve the soup.

Serving Suggestions:

✦ Chopped cilantro, lemon wedges, and your favorite hot sauce are nice additions to each bowl served.

✦ Corn or flour tortillas, as well as sliced avocados, are great accompaniments.

Beef Soup

Here's a slightly heartier version of the preceding soup.

Makes 4 to 6 servings

1 pound lean stewing beef, cubed	1 heaping teaspoon chopped garlic
2–2 1/2 pounds beef bones (shank bones with marrow are best)	3 1/2 cups bite-size chopped cabbage
3 quarts water	2 cups cubed potato
2 teaspoons salt	2 ears corn, cut into thirds or fourths
1 cup coarsely chopped celery	1 (16-ounce) can whole peeled tomatoes, crushed
1 cup coarsely chopped carrots	

Rinse the meat in cold water. In a stockpot, add the meat, bones, and salt to the water. Once the water begins to boil on high, reduce the heat and simmer uncovered for 2 hours. Continue to skim off the fat and floating debris as needed.

After 2 hours, remove the meat and bones. When the meat is cool enough to handle, remove and discard the bones, and return the meat to the pot; just be sure it's tender first.

Add all remaining ingredients, simmer for 1 hour, and serve.

Serving Suggestions:

✦ Chopped cilantro, lemon wedges, and your favorite hot sauce are nice additions to each bowl served.

✦ Corn or flour tortillas, as well as sliced avocados, are great accompaniments.

Matt Martinez's Culinary Frontier

Potato Soup

If you preheat your empty bowls a few minutes in a 180° oven, the soup will retain its heat much longer. You will especially appreciate this on freezing winter days.

Makes 4 to 6 servings

2 tablespoons butter

4 cups diced (1/4-inch) potatoes

1/2 cup coarsely chopped celery

1/2 cup coarsely chopped white onion

1 cup finely diced carrots

1 teaspoon salt

1/2 teaspoon black pepper

2 cups Chicken Broth (canned, or see page 47)

1 cup chopped cooked ham or brisket

3 cups milk

2 tablespoons chopped fresh flat-leaf parsley, for garnish

In a large pot, simmer the butter, potatoes, celery, onion, carrot, salt, pepper, and broth uncovered on low heat for 1 hour. Then, either mash the vegetables or leave them chunky (your preference). Add the ham or brisket, and the milk, and simmer for 15 minutes. Add additional broth or water, depending on how thick you like your soup.

Garnish with the parsley, and serve while hot.

You-Be-the-Judge Salads

Here's an easy formula for numerous salads, along with suggestions. Simply choose 1 main ingredient from column A, the dressing from column B, and vegetables from column C.

Make your selections, and spoon them over your favorite salad of fresh greens, tomatoes, cucumbers, etc.

Makes 1 serving

Main Ingredient

1 cup cooked and cubed:

Chicken

Shrimp

Fish

Turkey

Duck

Brisket

Roast beef

Roast pork

Beef tongue

Raw veggies

Cooked beans

Dressing

1/4 cup
equal parts
mayonnaise
and sour cream

Vegetables

1/4 cup chopped:

celery

or

(for brisket, tongue, roast beef, or pork) combine equal parts sour pickles and sweet white onion

In a bowl, combine all the ingredients you have selected, spoon them over salad greens, adjust salt and pepper to taste, and serve.

Serving Suggestions:

- ✦ I strongly encourage the use of smoked meats.
- ✦ My recommended garnishes are chopped onions, cilantro, and flat-leaf parsley.
- ✦ A squeeze of fresh lime may be added.
- ✦ Dark multi-grain bread was made for these salads.
- ✦ These salads (without the added greens) are also excellent stuffings for tomatoes—a summer favorite.

South Austin Three-Bean Salad

Long ago, when my parents included plate-lunch specials with their Tex-Mex dishes at the original El Rancho, I overheard my mother telling a helper to hurry to the store and buy some canned beans for a salad.

Well, I had never known anyone who put beans in a salad. I thought my mother had lost it. But it was a hit on the menu, and a hit with me, too.

Makes 8 to 10 servings

1 (15-ounce) can pinto beans	1 tablespoon Worcestershire sauce
1 (15-ounce) can red beans	1 cup finely chopped fresh cilantro leaves, loosely packed
1 (15-ounce) can Northern white beans	1 cup finely chopped white onions
1/4 cup red wine vinegar	1/2 cup seeded and finely chopped red or green bell pepper
2 tablespoons honey	1/2 cup finely chopped celery
2 tablespoons olive or vegetable oil	Chopped green onions and pickled jalapeños, for garnish
2 ounces tequila	
1/4 cup fresh lime juice	

Thoroughly mix all the ingredients except the garnish. Place them in a large air-tight plastic storage bag.

Refrigerate the salad for at least 1 hour before serving. Garnish it with the chopped green onions and pickled jalapeños.

Fisherman's Salad

Please take my word on this:

Everything in the Fisherman's Salad must—I repeat, MUST—be done in threes, or you'll have 3 months of bad-luck fishing.

Also, if you salt to taste, be sure to throw a pinch over your left shoulder with your right hand before seasoning.

Although this recipe calls for finely chopped onions, peppers, and celery, coarsely chopped is just as good if that's the way you like 'em.

Makes 3 servings (more, at your own risk)

3 (3¾-ounce) tins sardines in oil	3 tablespoons cider vinegar
⅓ cup finely chopped onion	3 small cloves garlic, crushed and finely chopped
⅓ cup finely chopped jalapeño or serrano chile peppers	⅓ teaspoon black pepper
⅓ cup finely chopped celery	Salt, to taste (optional)
3 tablespoons mustard (French's, no "foo-foo")	

Combine all the ingredients in a large bowl. Break up the sardines while blending. You may adjust salt to taste.

Serving Suggestions:
+ Eat Fisherman's Salad with crackers, celery sticks, or chips.
+ Use it as a sandwich spread, but only with white bread.

Matt's Jalapeño Coleslaw

I stumbled onto this recipe by accident. While making coleslaw with vinaigrette, I accidentally included some jalapeño juice in the vinaigrette.

I liked the taste so much I began incorporating jalapeños into the coleslaw. It's amazing how the jalapeños are an absolute natural with slaw. Today, I have a hard time eating coleslaw without jalapeños.

Makes 4 to 6 servings

1 small head green cabbage, or 1 (16 ounce) package coleslaw mix	2 tablespoons vegetable oil
1/3 cup sour cream	1 clove garlic, finely diced
1/3 cup mayonnaise	1/4 cup chopped pickled jalapeño
2 tablespoons red wine vinegar	Salt and black pepper, to taste

In a bowl, mix all the ingredients except the salt and pepper, and chill them. Just before serving, season to taste with salt and pepper.

Serving Suggestion:

+ Load up a pork, roast beef, or brisket sandwich with Jalapeño Coleslaw, and you won't need anything else on it.

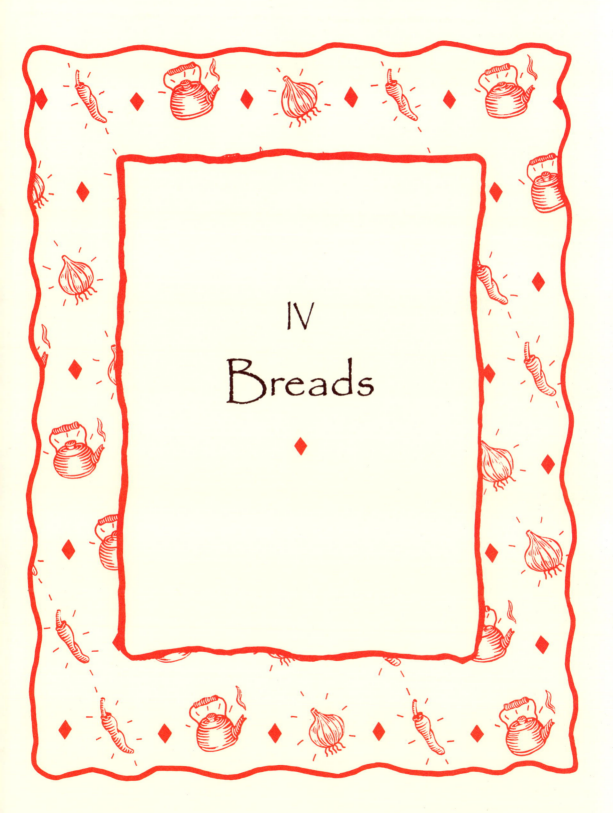

IV

Breads

◆

Early Texas Corn Bread

The cowboys of yesteryear basically stuck to regular ol' sourdough breads, biscuits, and corn breads. When you're out on the prairie like that and you've got your Dutch oven, the easiest thing to do is fix up some biscuits and corn bread.

This is real basic stuff, straight out of the saddle bags and into the stomach.

Makes 4 to 6 servings

1 1/2 cups yellow cornmeal	1 egg
1/2 cup flour	1/4 cup lard, bacon drippings, or vegetable shortening
2 teaspoons baking powder	
1 teaspoon salt	1 cup whole milk

Preheat the oven to 375°. Mix all the ingredients in a bowl. Grease a 12-inch baking pan, pour in the mix, and bake for about 20 minutes, until golden brown.

Crackling Corn Bread

Back in the old days, when there wasn't much meat available, the cowboys would cook up a mess of beans or chili and throw it down with some of this crackling corn bread.

Makes 4 to 6 servings

1 1/2   cups cornmeal

1/2   cup flour

2   teaspoons baking powder

1   teaspoon salt

1   egg

1/4   cup lard, bacon drippings, or vegetable shortening

1 1/4   cups buttermilk

1   cup crumbled cracklings or bacon

Preheat the oven to 375°. Mix all the ingredients in a bowl. Grease a 12-inch baking pan, pour in the mix, and bake for about 20 minutes, until golden brown.

Jalapeño Corn Bread

I prefer to give my corn bread a little kick, which explains the jalapeños and onions.

Makes 4 to 6 servings

1 1/2 cups cornmeal

1/2 cup flour

2 teaspoons baking powder

1 teaspoon salt

1 egg

1/4 cup lard, bacon drippings, or vegetable shortening

1 1/4 cups buttermilk

1/4 cup chopped jalapeño

1/2 cup finely chopped onion

1 cup grated Cheddar or Monterey Jack cheese

Preheat the oven to 375°. Mix all the ingredients in a bowl. Grease a 12-inch baking pan, pour in the mix, and bake for about 20 minutes, until golden brown.

Early Texas Biscuits

Although I list vegetable shortening for the next two biscuit recipes, it's best to use hog lard or bacon drippings.

Makes 12 to 14 biscuits

2 cups flour

1/2 teaspoon salt

1/2 teaspoon baking soda

1/4 cup lard, bacon drippings, or vegetable shortening

3/4 cup whole milk

While preheating the oven to 450°, grease a cookie sheet. Sift all the dry ingredients together in a bowl. Blend in the shortening and milk with a fork to obtain a cornmeal consistency (cowboys may use their hands).

Make a small foxhole in the center of the mixture, then knead lightly with your hands in a folding motion until it is thoroughly mixed.

On a floured board, pat out the dough or roll it out 1/4 to 1/2 inch thick. With a glass or a cookie cutter, cut out 1 1/2- to 2-inch circles and place them, 1/2-inch apart, on the cookie sheet. Bake until the biscuit tops are golden brown, 10 to 12 minutes.

Biscuits Unnamed

These biscuits are so basic, they don't need a name.

Makes 12 to 14 biscuits

- 2 cups flour
- 1 1/2 teaspoons sugar
- 1 tablespoon baking powder
- 1/4 cup lard, bacon drippings, or vegetable shortening
- 3/4 cup buttermilk

While preheating the oven to 450°, grease a cookie sheet. Sift all of the dry ingredients together in a bowl. Blend in the shortening and buttermilk with a fork to obtain a cornmeal consistency (again, cowboys are encouraged to use their hands).

Make a small foxhole in the center of the mixture, then knead lightly with your hands in a folding motion until it is thoroughly mixed.

On a floured board, pat out the dough or roll it out 1/4 to 1/2 inch thick. With a glass or cookie cutter, cut out 1 1/2- to 2-inch circles and place them, 1/2-inch apart, on the cookie sheet. Bake until the biscuit tops are golden brown, 10 to 12 minutes.

Flour Tortillas

In the morning, the smell of flour tortillas cooking ranks right up there with coffee brewing and bacon frying. It'll turn heads and whet the appetite big time.

Makes 12 to 14 tortillas

2	cups flour	1	cup water
2	teaspoons baking powder	2	teaspoons salt
1/4	pound lard or vegetable shortening		

In a bowl, mix the flour and baking powder. Thoroughly rub the lard or shortening into the flour. Heat the water to lukewarm (100–120°F.—not too hot) and dissolve the salt in it, then add the water to the flour mixture. Knead well for 2 to 3 minutes. Roll the flour into one big ball—about the size of a grapefruit. Cover it and allow it to rest (do not refrigerate) for at least 30 minutes (2 hours is best). Knead the dough one more time for a minute or 2. Form the dough into balls roughly 1½ inches in diameter. On a floured board, roll out the balls into circles as thin as possible.

Place the tortillas on a hot, greaseless griddle, preferably cast iron. Cook them on one side for 18 to 20 seconds, then flip them and cook them on the other side for 12 to 15 seconds.

The tortillas will start to bubble and brown. If one puffs up, simply press it down to take out the air.

Cover the tortillas with a clean kitchen towel—no dirty towels, please—to keep them warm until serving time.

Suggestions:

✦ Never use an oven or microwave when reheating a tortilla. Place the tortilla flat in a skillet, as if cooking it, for 1 to 2 minutes.

✦ To store in the freezer or refrigerator, place the tortillas flat—never folded—in air-tight plastic storage bags.

Fried Tortillas

Fried tortillas have many uses. They can be taco shells, chips for dipping, garnish for tortilla soup, or the backbone of nachos, chalupas, and tostadas compuestas.

Oil of your choice

Corn (page 87) or Flour Tortillas
(page 84)

For taco shells only: Pour the oil to a depth of 1½ to 2 inches in a large skillet, and heat to 375°. Place the whole tortilla in the middle of the hot oil. Mold the tortilla by pushing its center down with a metal spatula until the sides rise. Do not make your shells too tight or they will be difficult to fill without breaking. Fry until the tortillas are lightly browned. Drain and dab off the excess grease with paper towels.

For all fried tortillas, including taco shells: Fry the tortillas in the oil of your choice (lard is tastiest) at 375° until they reach the desired crispiness. I prefer them lightly browned.

When the tortillas are floating and the bubbles have slowed—in about 2 to 3 minutes—they're ready. Drain, and dab off the excess grease with paper towels.

Serving Suggestions:
+ Cut the tortillas into quarters before frying if you are going to use them as chips for dipping.
+ For nachos, cut the tortillas in half.
+ For tortilla soup garnish, cut them into thin strips.
+ For chalupas or tostadas compuestas, leave them whole.
+ Always drain and dab off the excess grease.

Plain Ol' Corncakes

I have included three corncake recipes in this cookbook, each in a different category. The Breakfast Corncakes (page 22) are cousins of pancakes. Another corncake recipe is with the Vegetables and Side Dishes.

Eat these plain ol' cakes the way you'd eat biscuits and butter. I love 'em with chili or beans spooned on top.

Makes 4 to 6 cakes

1/4 cup flour	2	tablespoons vegetable shortening
3/4 cup yellow cornmeal	1	egg
1/2 teaspoon baking soda	1	cup buttermilk
2 teaspoons salt		

In a bowl, combine all the ingredients except the egg and buttermilk. Mix thoroughly until the shortening is well distributed.

Add the egg and buttermilk, and thoroughly whisk the ingredients until blended, 3 to 4 minutes. Lightly coat a 12-inch skillet with grease and, over medium heat, pour the batter into the pan. Regrease the pan between cakes, and fry 'em and flip 'em just as you would pancakes, until they are golden brown. This will take about 2 to 3 minutes. For 4 cakes, use 1/2 cup of batter per cake; for 6 small cakes, use 1/3 cup.

Matt Martinez's Culinary Frontier

Traditional Masa

Thanks to the influence of the French and Spanish, Mexico has always had some nice bakeries. The Mexicans have always known the delights of masa.

This is the dough that allows you to make tortillas. If you're looking for a short-cut, buy masa harina and follow the instructions on the label.

Ground limestone can be purchased at any traditional Mexican grocery store or market. If you're having trouble finding dried corn kernels, I recommend a feedstore. Really.

Makes 4 dozen tortillas

2	pounds dried corn kernels	4	quarts water
2	tablespoons ground limestone		

Bring all the ingredients to a boil in a large pot. Cook uncovered over low heat, stirring occasionally (do not skim the floating residue), until the corn is tender yet still firm. This will take about $2^{1}/_{2}$ to 3 hours. Let the masa stand in the pot overnight.

Strain the corn through a sieve and grind it in a hand grinder. You may need to add some water while grinding. Knead the corn until a firm, smooth dough is obtained. You'll know it's ready when the dough smooths out.

Roll out the dough as you would a flour tortilla. Cook the masa in a hot dry skillet 2 to 3 minutes on each side, until the tortilla is firm.

The Martinez family on vacation in Monterrey, Mexico, in the 1950s. (Left to right) Gloria, Matt Jr., Matt Sr., Janie, and Sissy.

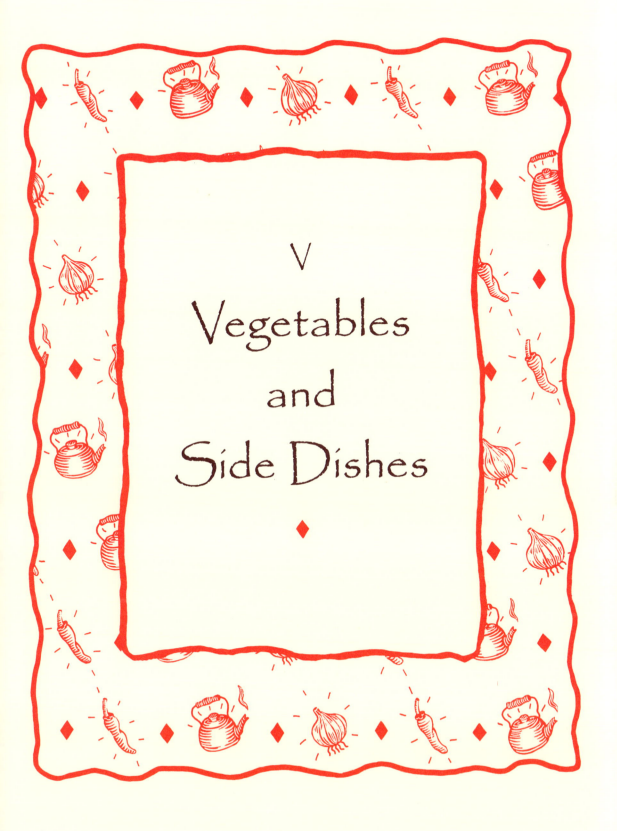

V

Vegetables
and
Side Dishes

Skillet-Style Onions

I don't like the sharpness of yellow onions. I prefer the consistent sweetness of the white ones. I like to take the biggest onion I can find and cut it the way I want for that particular meal, then I rinse it a little in cold water to bring out the sweetness. That's the kind of bite I like out of an onion.

Skillet-Style Onions are a side dish with no onion bite. They're good accompaniments for steaks, chicken, and fish, or as a garnish for hamburgers.

Makes 4 to 6 servings

- 4 cups coarsely chopped white onions
- 2 tablespoons salt
- 2 cups water
- 1/4 cup distilled white vinegar
- 2 tablespoons olive oil

- 2 teaspoons Texas Sprinkle (page 42)
- 1 teaspoon cornstarch
- 2 tablespoons Black Magic Finishing Sauce (page 41)
- 1/4 cup butter

In a plastic container, soak the onions in the salt, water, and vinegar for 10 to 15 minutes. Thoroughly drain the onions and pat them dry with a clean kitchen towel.

In a skillet, heat the oil to smoking (375°). Add the onions and sauté for 30 seconds. Add the Texas Sprinkle and cornstarch, and sauté for 30 seconds. Add the Black Magic and sauté for 5 to 10 seconds.

Remove the skillet from the heat. Add the butter, and continue stirring just until the butter melts. Serve immediately.

Skillet-Style Portobello Mushrooms

In my youth, my pals and I ate no mushrooms because we believed every one of them was poisonous. We'd be walking along and somebody would shout, "Oh my gosh! Look! A mushroom!" And we'd all walk around it. Most of the ones we saw in the fields probably were pretty gross.

I remember once we had something in school that had canned mushrooms in it, a stew or something, and I told everyone, "Don't eat those mushrooms! They're poisonous!"

I meant it, too, at the time. By then, my friends knew I was serious about cooking, so everybody backed off. A lot of good mushrooms went to waste at our table.

Absolutely my favorite mushrooms for cooking are the portobellos from Italy, but they're growing them now in Texas, too.

Portobellos are so meaty. They're full and firm and have great flavor. They respond to just about any cooking technique.

I also like the little saki mushrooms, the dry mushrooms, I'll work with any mushroom I have to, but by far, portobellos are the best.

Makes 4 to 6 servings

1/4 cup thinly sliced garlic	1 tablespoon cornstarch
1 tablespoon salt	1/4 cup butter
1 cup water	Juice of 1/2 fresh lemon
2 tablespoons olive oil	2 ounces dry vermouth
1 cup coarsely chopped white onions	
8 ounces portobello mushrooms, coarsely chopped	

In a bowl, soak the sliced garlic in the salt and water for 10 to 15 minutes, then drain. Heat the olive oil to smoking (375°). Add the onions and sauté for 30 seconds. Add the mushrooms and sauté for 30 seconds more.

Matt Martinez's Culinary Frontier

Reduce the heat to low. Sprinkle in the cornstarch, and immediately add the drained garlic and butter. Sauté for 5 or 6 minutes. Add the lemon juice and vermouth, and sauté for another 30 seconds. Serve immediately.

Serving Suggestion:

✦ Cook 8 ounces of pasta and toss with the mushrooms. Sprinkle with chopped fresh flat-leaf parsley and freshly grated Parmesan cheese.

Sister Sissy (left), Kathy, mother Janie, and sister Gloria, each with a pet. The dog was one of Matt's favorites, Bunny.

Vegetarian Drunk Beans

Not me, Granny, my mother, not anybody in our family soaks beans. We still do 'em the way Granny Gaytan did every single time for all those years, using the same 4-quart, red clay pot.

You could pick Granny's pot up off the fire by grabbing its two little ol' ears. Her pot had a lid that didn't fit real good, and the bottom was black from sitting over so many gas stove fires.

I've gone in search of many makes of beans from every single store I can imagine, and I've used every soaking method I've known—a dry soak, a fast soak, a salt soak, a hot-water soak. But whenever I put out my regular ol' beans that have never been soaked? That's when I get the best flavor.

Back in the old days, they'd carry beans around sometimes for five years. Well, of course, they're going to be dried.

Today's beans aren't as dry. My granny and mother have always stressed using fresh products. My granny grew her own beans and kept them in a gallon jar with the lid on. They never dried out, and they never needed soaking.

Although the following bean recipes call for pintos, feel free to use black beans, white Northern beans, or black-eyed peas instead. The black beans will take about an hour longer than the pintos; Northern and black-eyed peas will cook about an hour faster than pintos.

Make 6 to 8 servings

- 1 pound (2 cups) pinto beans
- 6 cups water
- 1 cup coarsely chopped white onions
- 1 cup coarsely chopped celery
- 1 cup coarsely chopped green or red bell peppers
- 2 cloves garlic, crushed and finely chopped
- 1/2 small bay leaf
- 1 large whole zucchini
- 1 cup coarsely chopped fresh cilantro, loosely packed
- 1/2 bottle or can Lone Star beer

  Salt and black pepper, to taste

While drinking the half of the beer you won't be using in the recipe, put all the other ingredients into a large pot and bring it to a boil. Just throw the whole zucchini into the pot. Cover and simmer on low heat for 2 hours.

Then add the beer you haven't already swallowed.

Simmer on low heat for another 30 minutes to an hour, until the beans are tender. Season with the salt and pepper.

Serving Suggestion:

+ The zucchini adds a special sweetness to these beans. When serving, cut off a piece of zucchini for each bowl of beans.

Cowboy Matt's first horse ride

Cowboy Open-Range Beans No. 1

These make for a hearty Southwestern side dish, but they were an evening meal for many a lonely cowboy. Corn-bread biscuits or white bread are natural bean pals.

Makes 6 to 8 servings

4	slices of uncooked bacon	6	cups water
1	pound (2 cups) pinto beans		Salt and black pepper, to taste

Slice the bacon into bite-size pieces. Combine it with the beans and water in a pot large enough to accommodate a small posse of hungry cowboys.

Bring the water to a boil, then cover it, and simmer on low heat. Cooking time usually varies between $2\frac{1}{2}$ and $3\frac{1}{2}$ hours. Keep the beans covered with liquid by adding water 1 cup at a time as needed.

Add the salt and pepper at the end of the cooking time.

Cowboy Open-Range Beans No. 2

The difference between Cowboy Open-Range Beans 1 and 2 is that this recipe is a bit more complicated. You get to throw in more stuff.

Makes 6 to 8 servings

4 slices of uncooked bacon	1/2 small bay leaf (optional)
1 pound (2 cups) pinto beans	2 cups Beef Broth (page 48), or 1 (15-ounce) can beef broth
6 cups water	
2 cloves garlic, crushed	2 tablespoons chili powder
1 cup coarsely chopped onions	Salt and black pepper, to taste

Slice the bacon into bite-size pieces. Combine it with the beans and all other ingredients except the salt and pepper in an adequate-sized pot.

Bring the water to a boil, then cover and simmer on low heat. Cooking time usually varies between 2¹/₂ and 3¹/₂ hours. Keep the beans covered with liquid by adding 1 cup of water at a time as needed.

Add the salt and pepper at the end of the cooking time.

Spicy Charro Beans

This is a variation of a dish served on the open prairies of the Southwest more than a century ago. Cowboys put whatever they had in their beans and often ate them many days in a row, each time enjoying different tastes. It's hard to get bored when you keep adding a little of this, a little of that.

Makes 6 to 8 servings

1 pound (2 cups) pinto beans	2 cups diced fresh tomatoes
6 cups water	4 whole fresh jalapeños
1 pound Simple Chorizo (page 32)	1 cup chopped fresh cilantro, loosely packed
2 cloves garlic, crushed	
1 cup finely chopped onions	

In a large pot, bring the beans and water to a boil. Cover the pot and simmer the beans on low heat.

After 1 hour, sauté the Simple Chorizo in a skillet. Add the garlic, onions, and tomatoes to the chorizo and sauté for 2 to 3 minutes more, until the onions are translucent, then add this mixture to the bean pot along with the jalapeños and cilantro.

Cover the pot and cook over low heat until the beans are tender. This should take 1½ to 2 hours more.

When the beans are ready, crush open the jalapeños one at a time with a spoon against the side of the pot. Continue breaking the jalapeños until you reach the spiciness you desire. Remove any remaining jalapeños.

Serving Suggestion:

✚ Leftover jalapeños may be crushed into a small bowl and used by those who prefer spicier beans.

Refried Beans

Refried Beans are much better if you use bacon drippings or hog lard. Vegetable oil may be substituted, but you'll lose the flavor if you do. The cheese also enhances the overall flavor.

Makes 4 to 6 servings

1/4 cup bacon drippings or hog lard

4 cups cooked Cowboy Open-Range Beans No. 1 (page 96),

1 cup grated Monterey Jack or American cheese (optional)

Get the drippings or lard smoking hot in a heavy skillet. Carefully add 1 cup of the cooked beans for 1 minute, and mash them. Add the remaining beans, turn the heat to low, and continue mashing until the beans are smooth and creamy. This will take about 15 to 20 minutes.

If you prefer drier beans (they're still good), cook them another 10 to 15 minutes.

Serve the refried beans as they are, or sprinkle the cheese over them after mashing all the beans. Allow the cheese to melt into the beans before serving.

Corncakes as a Side Dish

You could put up a good argument that corncakes are bread and therefore should be listed with the other breads. I'll even admit that the following corncakes go better than hush puppies with fried fish.

But hear me out on this. The filling gives these cakes enough variety to make them a combination sweet bread and side dish rolled into one.

Use your imagination—and your leftovers—to concoct any combination that makes you happy. Just be sure to stay with the measurements.

Makes 4 to 6 cakes

1/4 cup flour	1 egg
3/4 cup yellow cornmeal	1 cup buttermilk
1/2 teaspoon baking soda	1 cup filling of your choice (see Suggestions below)
1/2 teaspoon salt	
2 tablespoons vegetable shortening, plus extra for the pan	

In a bowl, combine all the ingredients except the egg, buttermilk, and filling. Mix thoroughly until the shortening is well distributed.

Add the egg and buttermilk, and thoroughly whisk the ingredients until everything is blended. Mix in the filling.

Lightly coat a skillet with vegetable shortening and, over medium heat, pour the batter into the pan. Use 1/2 cup of batter per cake and grease the pan between cakes. Fry 'em and flip 'em just as you would pancakes, until your corncakes are golden brown. Serve hot.

Filling Suggestions:

✦ Combine 1/3 cup each finely chopped pickled jalapeño, coarsely chopped sweet white onion, and the shredded cheese of your choice.

Matt Martinez's Culinary Frontier

✤ Combine $1/3$ cup *each* finely chopped tomato, coarsely chopped white or green onion, and shredded Monterey Jack or American cheese.

✤ For breakfast or as a side dish for beans, use $1/3$ cup *each* crumbled cooked sausage, diced hot peppers, and shredded cheese; *or,* $1/2$ cup shredded cooked beef and $1/2$ cup shredded American cheese; *or,* $1/2$ cup crumbled chorizo and $1/2$ cup shredded Monterey Jack cheese.

✤ If you are using spinach or cabbage, use $1 1/2$ cups, chopped and loosely packed.

✤ If using carrots, chop them very fine.

✤ For a quick stuffing, use $1/3$ cup *each* finely chopped green onion, celery, and green bell pepper.

Spanish Rice

For more flavor, at the beginning of the cooking time add a heaping teaspoon of chopped fresh flat-leaf parsley or cilantro to this recipe.

Or, 2 cups of any raw vegetable may be added while bringing the water or broth to a boil. The old way of cooking may at first seem extremely basic, but it's up to you to be creative. Dabble, and come up with the combinations of your choice.

Makes 4 to 6 servings

3 tablespoons vegetable oil or shortening	2 teaspoons ground cumin
1 1/2 cups uncooked long-grain rice	1 1/2 teaspoons granulated garlic
1/2 cup finely chopped onion	1/2 teaspoon black pepper
1/4 cup finely chopped celery	3 cups water, or Chicken Broth (canned, or see page 47)
1/4 cup finely chopped green bell pepper	1 (8-ounce) can tomato sauce
1 teaspoon salt	

Heat the oil in a skillet and sauté the rice until it is golden brown. Add the vegetables and seasonings, and continue to sauté for 1 to 2 minutes longer.

Add the water or broth and the tomato sauce, and bring to a boil. Cover and simmer for 15 minutes.

Remove the rice from the heat and let it stand 3 to 4 minutes, still covered.

Fluff and serve.

Steamed Rice

The old Chinese belly-filler goes beautifully with shrimp, fish, meats, and as a bed for grilled vegetables.

Makes 4 to 6 servings

1 1/2   cups long-grain rice

3   cups water or Chicken Broth (canned, or see page 47)

3   tablespoons butter or vegetable oil (butter is best)

Pinch of salt (optional, but recommended if not using broth)

Combine all the ingredients in a 2-quart pot and bring to a boil. Cover, and simmer on low heat for 15 minutes. Do not lift the lid during cooking.

Remove the pan from the heat and let the rice sit, covered, for 3 to 4 minutes.

Fluff and serve.

Optional:

◆ As with the Spanish Rice, for more flavoring add a heaping teaspoon of chopped fresh parsley or cilantro at the beginning of the cooking period. Or, 2 cups of any raw vegetable may be added while bringing the water or broth to a boil.

Fideo (Vermicelli as a Side Dish)

You'll find another fideo in the "Light and Main Courses" section. That one includes meat and fills up the plate a little more. This one is great with fowl, meats, and seafood. For even more taste, sprinkle it with freshly grated Parmesan cheese or chopped fresh cilantro.

Makes 4 to 6 servings

- 3 tablespoons vegetable oil or bacon drippings
- 1 (5-ounce) box vermicelli
- 1/2 teaspoon salt
- 1/4 teaspoon black pepper
- 3/4 teaspoon granulated garlic
- 1 teaspoon ground cumin
- 1/2 cup coarsely chopped white onion
- 1/4 cup coarsely chopped green bell pepper
- 1/4 cup tomato sauce
- 2 cups water, or Chicken Broth (canned, or see page 47)

Heat the oil or drippings in a skillet to medium heat, add the vermicelli, and stir constantly for 3 to 4 minutes, until the vermicelli is golden brown. Add the spices and vegetables and stir 1 minute.

Add the water or broth and the tomato sauce. Simmer on low heat for 7 to 8 minutes, until the vermicelli is bitey-tender, but still firm. Serve right away.

Hunter's Cabbage

This and the following two are my favorite cabbage recipes. Each has its own distinctive flavor. All are good over steamed rice, or make an excellent side dish for meat, seafood, or chicken.

Makes 4 to 6 servings

4 slices of bacon	1/2 head (about 6 cups) coarsely chopped green cabbage
3 tablespoons reserved drippings from the bacon	1 cup water
1 cup coarsely chopped onions	1 tablespoon distilled white vinegar
1 tablespoon flour	1 teaspoon sugar
1 teaspoon crushed and finely chopped garlic	

Fry the bacon until crisp, then remove it from the pan to drain on paper towels, and reserve 3 tablespoons of the drippings. Crumble the bacon. In the drippings, fry the onions for 3 to 4 minutes, or until they're lightly browned. Add the flour, garlic, and crumbled bacon, and sauté for 1 minute, taking care not to brown the garlic.

Add the cabbage, water, vinegar, and sugar. Simmer uncovered until the cabbage is tender, 15 to 20 minutes. Serve hot.

Mexican-Style Cabbage

Remember, in the old days cowboys often used whatever was available. Therefore, jerky, shredded meats, ham, or sausage may be used in this dish instead of the bacon. Also, the oil of your choice may be substituted for the drippings.

Makes 4 to 6 servings

- 4 slices of bacon
- 3 tablespoons reserved drippings from the bacon
- 1 cup coarsely chopped white onions
- 1/2 cup coarsely chopped red or green bell pepper
- 1/2 teaspoon salt, plus extra, to taste
- 1/4 teaspoon black pepper, plus extra, to taste

- 3/4 teaspoon crushed and finely chopped garlic
- 1 teaspoon ground cumin
- 1 tablespoon flour
- 1/2 head (about 6 cups) coarsely chopped green cabbage
- 1 cup water, or Chicken Broth (canned, or see page 47)
- 1 (8-ounce) can tomato sauce

In a skillet, fry the bacon until crispy and transfer it to drain on paper towels, leaving 3 tablespoons of drippings in the pan. Sauté the onions, bell pepper, and seasonings in the drippings for 3 to 4 minutes.

When the onions are fully cooked, add the flour and continue cooking over moderate heat for 1 minute. Add the cabbage, as well as the water or broth, and the tomato sauce. Also, crumble up the bacon you have reserved and add it.

Simmer the cabbage uncovered over low heat, stirring occasionally, for 15 to 20 minutes, until it reaches the desired tenderness. Season with additional salt and pepper to taste. Serve piping hot.

Serving Suggestions:
- ✦ Serve the cabbage over steamed rice.
- ✦ Serve it as a side dish with meat, seafood, or chicken.

Dilled Cabbage

I particularly like a hint of dill taste with dove, quail, duck, wild boar, or any wild game.

Makes 4 to 6 servings

- 4 tablespoons butter
- 1 teaspoon crushed and finely chopped garlic
- 1 cup coarsely chopped onions
- 1/2 head (about 6 cups) coarsely chopped green cabbage

- 1 cup water
- 1 teaspoon sugar
- 1 tablespoon finely chopped fresh dill pickle
- 1 tablespoon fresh lemon juice

In a skillet, melt the butter, and sauté the garlic and onions over low heat for 2 to 3 minutes, until the onions are translucent but not browned. Add the remaining ingredients.

Cover the pan and steam on low heat until the cabbage reaches the desired tenderness, 15 to 20 minutes. Serve immediately.

Corn on the Cob (The Right Way)

Everybody murders corn on the cob by trying to do too much to it. The essences of early summer are the early crops of good tomatoes and corn. Why intrude on these wonderful delicacies?

Corn should be cooked enough to sweeten the water with a little juice from the corn. Add butter, salt, and pepper, and thank the Lord for the simple things in life.

Makes 1 serving

    1   ear of corn

Shuck the fresh corn. Cut off the ends and rinse off the silk. Place the corn in a pot and cover it with water. Bring the water to a boil and allow it to continue boiling for 1 minute before turning off the heat.

Cover the pot and let the corn stand for 5 to 7 minutes. Drain off the excess water and serve the corn immediately, piping hot.

Serving Suggestions:

+ Garnish the corn with butter at room temperature, salt, and pepper, or with freshly grated Parmesan cheese and lemon slices.

+ Summertime corn is an easy snack or light lunch with cold beer.

Barbecued Corn

This same technique may be used with zucchini squash. Simply quarter the squash crosswise and follow the directions below for a very tasty surprise.

Makes 1 serving

- 1 ear of corn, shucked

- 1/2 teaspoon Texas Sprinkle (page 42)

- 1 tablespoon butter, at room temperature

- 1 tablespoon prepared barbecue sauce

Rub the corn first with the Texas Sprinkle, next with the butter, and last with the barbecue sauce.

Wrap the ear of corn in aluminum foil. Roast it over medium coals for 10 to 15 minutes, turning it frequently, until the corn is slightly tender. Or roast in a 350° oven for 20 to 30 minutes.

Once slightly tender, move the corn to a corner of the grill away from the direct flame. Let it rest and continue to tenderize while preparing the rest of your meal. When you're ready to eat, unwrap the foil and serve the corn hot.

Serving Suggestion:
+ Barbecued corn goes well with any other barbecued items and is great for summer picnics.

Baked Corn

This is a creamier, richer version of corn. Obviously, not everything on your plate has to be spicy in order to add some zip to your meal. Try adding ¹/₄ cup chopped pickled jalapeño before baking to give you the spicy flavor you want with a grilled, unseasoned steak, and a fresh salad.

Makes 4 to 6 servings

2 eggs	3 cups grated American cheese
¹/₂ cup whole milk	1 teaspoon black pepper
1 (14.5-ounce) can corn kernels	¹/₄ cup bacon drippings (best), vegetable oil, or butter
1 (14.5-ounce) can creamed corn	¹/₄ cup chopped pickled jalapeño, optional
¹/₂ cup cornmeal	
1 tablespoon flour	
1 teaspoon salt	

Preheat the oven to 350°. In a bowl, thoroughly beat the eggs and combine them with the milk. Pour the mixture into a 12 × 14 inch baking pan, and add all the remaining ingredients, including the jalapeño, if desired.

Bake for 45 to 50 minutes, until the ingredients firm and cake up.

Fried Okra

In the summer months when okra is at its best, we Texans are known to enjoy okra stewed with tomatoes, or battered and fried. I like 'em good and crunchy.

Makes 4 to 6 servings

1 pound fresh okra, or 2 packages frozen okra	1 1/2 cups yellow cornmeal
1/2 cup water (beer may be substituted)	1 teaspoon salt
	1/2 teaspoon black pepper
2 tablespoons cornstarch	1/2 cup vegetable oil
1 egg	

Cut the okra into 1/2-inch-thick rounds (or buy it precut). In a bowl, combine the water (or beer), cornstarch, and egg, and whisk vigorously. Thoroughly coat the okra in the mixture.

In a paper sack, combine the cornmeal, salt, and pepper. Vigorously shake the sack, mixing the ingredients (no hip motion is necessary). Place the okra in the sack and shake it vigorously again, until each piece of okra is coated with cornmeal.

In a large skillet, heat the oil to 350°. Fry the okra in the oil, turning the pieces frequently, until golden brown. This will take 3 to 4 minutes.

Each time a few are golden to taste, remove them to drain on paper towels. Eat 'em while they're hot.

Fried Eggplant

If you love eggplant, you already know it's a great side dish for almost any main course.

Makes 4 servings

1 eggplant	1 teaspoon salt
1 egg	1/2 teaspoon black pepper
1/2 cup whole milk	1/2 cup vegetable oil
1 1/2 cups cornmeal or cracker meal	

Wash and peel the eggplant, then cut it into 1/2-inch-thick rounds.

In a bowl, whisk together the egg and milk. Add the eggplant and thoroughly coat it in the egg mixture.

In a paper sack, combine the cornmeal, salt, and pepper. Vigorously shake the sack to combine the ingredients. Place the eggplant in the sack and vigorously shake it again, until the eggplant is coated with cornmeal.

Heat the oil to 350° in a large skillet and fry the eggplant until it is golden brown. This will take 3 to 4 minutes.

Drain the eggplant on paper towels, and serve it immediately.

Smoked Baked Potato

In frontier days, cowboys would throw a few potatoes into the campfire before falling asleep. The next day, breakfast was ready.

When we're planning on going hunting, my friends and I always see eye to eye on this particular part of the preparations: Each of us stuffs a potato in his or her pants pocket, if for no other reason than to always have something to eat.

Sometimes we bury the potatoes in the coals and off we go hunting, often for hours. I always carry a little salt and pepper in a pillbox or in wax paper. We peel off the burned portions of the potato with a stick or a knife and eat the rest.

Using a smoker or barbecue pit, cook the potato dry (do not oil the skin or wrap the potato in foil). Smoke it completely off the fire, at 225° indirect heat, for 3 to 3$^1/_2$ hours, or until the potato is tender.

Optional:

◆ For an even more intense smoke flavor, wrap the potato in cellophane and refrigerate it for a day before cooking. Remember, do not oil or wrap the potato when cooking.

Leftovers:

Left-over smoked baked potatoes, peeled and cubed, are good for:

✚ potato salad

✚ mashed potatoes

✚ potato soups and chowders

✚ sliced cold, with vinaigrette.

Matt's Stewed Potatoes

Seeded jalapeños make these potatoes an outstanding, flavorful side dish for steaks.

Makes 4 to 5 servings

1 cup oil of your choice (not olive)	2 tablespoons Black Magic Finishing Sauce (page 41)
2 large (approximately 2 pounds total) potatoes, diced or sliced 1/2 inch thick	1 (8-ounce) can tomato sauce
1 cup coarsely chopped onions	1 (8-ounce) can water
3–4 jalapeños, quartered, seeded if desired	1 teaspoon ground cumin
2 teaspoons Texas Sprinkle (page 42)	1 cup shredded Monterey Jack or American cheese (optional)
	Salt and black pepper, to taste

In a large skillet, heat the oil to hot. Splash 1 or 2 droplets of water in a corner of the skillet; if it "spits" back, the oil is ready. This usually takes 6 to 8 minutes. Add the potatoes and fry them 6 to 8 minutes, until golden brown. Remove the potatoes from the skillet with a slotted spoon, and drain them on paper towels. Discard the oil.

Sauté the onion and jalapeños in the same skillet without oil for about 1 minute.

Add the drained potatoes and the Texas Sprinkle, and continue to sauté for 2 to 3 minutes, until the onions are translucent.

Splash on the Black Magic and toss the ingredients.

Add the tomato sauce, water, and cumin. Simmer the potatoes for another 3 to 4 minutes, until the sauce bubbles.

Fold in the cheese (if desired), and season with the salt and pepper. Serve immediately.

Matt's Fries

What we have here are basic french fries, as we Texans call 'em, except the fries are all dressed up in jalapeños and onion. Which means, of course, that they're not so basic, after all. But they are flavorful and easy to make. They flatter steaks and hamburgers.

Makes 4 to 6 servings

1 cup oil of your choice (not olive)	2 teaspoons Texas Sprinkle (page 42)
2 large (approximately 2 pounds total) potatoes, diced or sliced 1/2 inch thick	2 tablespoons Black Magic Finishing Sauce (page 41)
1 cup coarsely chopped onions	
3–4 jalapeños, quartered	

In a large skillet, heat the oil to hot. To test the oil the old cowboy way, spit into a corner of the skillet (or splash in a couple of drops of water); if the oil "spits" back, it's hot enough. This usually takes 6 to 8 minutes.

Add the potatoes and fry them 6 to 8 minutes, to a crispy, golden brown. When the potatoes are done, remove them with a slotted spoon and drain them on paper towels. Remove the oil from the skillet.

Add the onions and jalapeños to the skillet, and sauté them without oil for approximately 1 minute.

Add the drained potatoes and Texas Sprinkle, and continue to sauté for 2 to 3 minutes, until the onions are translucent. Splash on the Black Magic, toss for 30 seconds, and serve.

Fettucini Martinez

The heck with Alfredo. This is a great side dish with steak, chicken, fish, or Cowboy Open-Range Beans Nos. 1 and 2 (pages 96 and 97).

Makes 4 servings

4 tablespoons butter	1/4 cup heavy cream
1/2 cup chopped onion	2 cups grated American cheese
1/4 cup chopped fresh jalapeño or serrano chile pepper	10 ounces fettucini, cooked according to package directions (but do not add salt or oil to the water)
1/4 cup chopped celery	
1/2 cup Chicken Broth (canned, or see page 47)	

Melt the butter in a skillet over very low heat. Add all the vegetables and sauté for 1 minute; the onion does not have to be translucent.

Add the broth and cream, and bring to a boil on high heat. When the liquid starts to boil, add the cheese and stir for 30 seconds.

Pour this sauce into an oven-proof serving dish. Add the cooked fettucini to the sauce, toss, and serve immediately.

Optional:

♦ Shell pasta or spaghetti may be substituted for the fettucini and is just as good.

♦ Red or green bell peppers may be substituted for the hot peppers if you don't want the fire in your mouth.

♦ When sautéing the vegetables, add 1 cup peas or black olives for more texture and color.

♦ Garnish with fresh cilantro or flat-leaf parsley.

♦ Sprinkle some Romano or Parmesan cheese over the fettucini just before serving.

Fried Peaches

If you really want to dazzle your guests, try this side dish with pork chops, pork roast, or any wild game. Your diners will leave the table still raving about it.

Makes 3 to 6 servings

- 3   ripe peaches, peeled
- 3   tablespoons butter
- 6   teaspoons brown sugar

- 1/4   tablespoon ground cinnamon (optional)
- Juice of 1/2 fresh lemon

Cut the peaches in half, removing the stones. Melt the butter in a skillet on low heat. Add the peaches, cut side down, for 1 minute. Flip over.

Sprinkle the sugar and, if desired (I do), the cinnamon evenly over the peaches. Fry for 10 to 15 minutes on low heat, basting the peaches with the butter. Right before serving, squeeze the lemon over the peaches.

Skillet Spinach

This is the way we make fresh spinach at my No Place restaurant in Dallas. Customers love it with just about any main course, or even on an all-vegetable platter. It's great—providing you like spinach. Even if you don't, try it; you might be surprised.

Makes 4 to 6 servings

- 4   slices of bacon
- 4   tablespoons bacon drippings (best) or butter
- 1   cup coarsely chopped onions
- 1   tablespoon Texas Sprinkle (page 42)
- 1   tablespoon flour

- 20   ounces spinach, stemmed and thoroughly washed
- 1/4   cup water or Chicken Broth (canned, or see page 47)
- 2   tablespoons Black Magic Finishing Sauce (page 41)

    Juice of 1 fresh lemon

In a skillet, fry the bacon, then drain, crumble, and reserve it. Discard all but 4 tablespoons of the drippings from the skillet; or, discard the drippings entirely and melt the butter over medium heat. Sauté the onions for 2 to 3 minutes, until translucent. Add the Texas Sprinkle, flour, and crumbled bacon. Sauté for approximately 1 minute, or until the flour starts to brown. Add half the spinach, tossing it with the onion and bacon crumbs for 30 seconds to 1 minute, until the spinach begins to wilt.

Add the remaining spinach along with the water or broth. Continue to toss while cooking. Also, pull the spinach from the bottom of the skillet and lay it on top, continuing in that fashion 1 1/2 to 2 minutes, until all the spinach is bright green and fully cooked. Add the Black Magic, and toss for 15 to 30 seconds. Squeeze the lemon juice on top, and serve immediately.

Optional:
- ◆ For sweeter spinach, add 2 tablespoons more butter when adding the second batch of spinach.
- ◆ I love to sprinkle Romano cheese over the spinach just before serving.

Vegetable Fajitas

Perhaps I should call these "Vegetables for Fajitas," because this is as much an "inside" dish as a side dish. Whenever making fajitas with meat, I always include Vegetable Fajitas with my meat, pico, queso, etc., inside the soft, rolled-up tortillas.

This recipe is also adequate for a light lunch—maybe even a whole meal for the vegetarian-inclined.

Makes 4 servings

2 tablespoons vegetable oil	1 teaspoon cornstarch
1 cup combination white onion and red or green bell pepper, chopped 1/2 inch thick	1 teaspoon Texas Sprinkle (page 42)
1 cup zucchini, chopped 1/2 inch thick	2 teaspoons Black Magic Finishing Sauce (page 41)
1 cup yellow squash, chopped 1/2 inch thick	1/4 cup water or Chicken Broth (canned, or see page 47)
1 cup corn kernels	

In a skillet, heat the oil to smoking hot. Toss the vegetables, cornstarch, and Texas Sprinkle in the hot skillet for about 1 minute. Add the Black Magic and the water or broth, and continue to mix thoroughly and toss for 30 to 45 seconds. Total cooking time should be about 1 1/2 to 2 minutes. Serve immediately.

Serving Suggestions:

✦ If eating Vegetable Fajitas without meat, load a soft tortilla with the cooked vegetables and wrap. Also, fill with such other sides as: hot sauce of your choice, Traditional Guacamole (page 62), Pico de Gallo (page 46), Chile con Queso (page 59), and tomatoes.

✦ Refried Beans (page 99) are a great side dish for fajitas.

VI
Light and
Main Courses

◆

Tostados Compuestas
(Estella's First Meal at El Rancho)

One day when I was 21, I got into a squabble with some guy in a bar. Before I knew it, we were rolling around in the gravel parking lot outside. It might have been okay, except his buddy came out, and either he started kicking me, or my ribs accidentally kept getting in the way of his boots.

That laid me up for about a week, and even then the ribs still looked bruised and ugly.

While recuperating, I received a phone call from my friend Jerry.

"Man, I just left the Jade Room," he said. "There's a good lookin' Mexican girl there you need to meet."

"I'm too sore," I complained. "I'm still feeling poorly from the last time we did something together."

Jerry persisted, and so, of course, I went with him.

The Jade Room was an Austin tavern on the Guadalupe Street drag near the University of Texas campus. The moment Jerry and I walked in, he nodded toward a table of teen-age girls. I took one look at Estella, who was about 18, and I thought, "Goodness gracious, look at that child!"

There was a guy talking to her, so Jerry and I bided our time at one end of the bar. When the guy went to the men's room, I followed.

"You know that girl you're talking to?" I asked the guy at the stall.

He smiled and said, "Her name's Estella, and she sure is purty."

"She sure is," I said. "But you see those bikers sitting nearby? Those girls belong to those bikers."

The guy gave me a peculiar look, so I pulled up my shirt and showed him my busted ribs.

"This is what those bikers did to me last week, and all I did was buy her a Coke."

I don't think he even finished what he was doing. He fled out the back door, never to be seen again.

I went over to the table and explained to the girls that an emergency had forced my "buddy" to rush off. That's when I gazed into Estella's eyes for the first time.

The girls invited me to sit down, but I was almost seated anyway. After being around Estella for 20 minutes, all I knew is I wanted to be with her some more.

The girls decided to go to another bar, and I asked the one with the car if I could go with them.

"No room," she said. "There's five of us and all I have is a little Valiant."

As they were pulling out, I spied an open back window. I took a little ol' runnin' jump and dived into the back seat on top of three of those girls.

I almost died. My ribs were hurting so bad, I had tears running down my face and I was gasping. I could hardly talk, but I managed to say, "Where we going?"

"To the Hook 'Em Lounge," the driver said.

Well, the girl I was dating at the time was a go-go dancer at the Hook 'Em, and she did not appear all that pleased when I walked through the door with five young women.

Later that night, Estella and I went to a small coffee shop and ate breakfast. I told her I was going to marry her and therefore we ought to have lunch the next day at my parents' restaurant.

She showed up, and—man!—she looked just as pretty as she did the night before. I couldn't believe it.

The first meal Estella ate at El Rancho were these Tostados Compuestas. We were served by Lupe, a waitress who's been with us since 1952. It was a great lunch. Five months later, Estella and I were married. There's never been any doubt in my mind that she was the one for me.

Now, we've got four grown children, a bushel of grandchildren, and we're still going strong.

To this day, when I get serious about cooking something, I pretend I'm cooking for Estella. I love her tremendously, and she's probably my biggest critic. Consequently, I cook with a lot of love. I am also incredibly careful not to make any mistakes.

Makes 6 to 10 tostados compuestas

For the Meat:

- 1 pound ground beef
- 1 teaspoon salt
- 2 teaspoons ground cumin
- 1 1/2 teaspoons granulated garlic
- 1/2 teaspoon black pepper

- 1/4 cup finely chopped onion
- 3 tablespoons finely chopped celery
- 3 tablespoons finely chopped green bell pepper

For the Rest:

1 taco shell per tostado compuesta,
   flat-fried (for frying the shell,
   see page 85)

1 heaping tablespoon grated
   Monterey Jack or American
   cheese

2 tablespoons Ranchero Salsa
   (page 31) or Tomatillo Salsa
   (page 30)

Combine the meat ingredients in a 10-inch skillet, and sauté over medium heat for 4 to 5 minutes, until the meat is thoroughly cooked. Remove from the heat.

Warm a flat-fried taco shell in the oven at low heat for 2 to 3 minutes. Spoon 1^1/$_2$ tablespoons of the taco meat onto the warm shell. Sprinkle on the cheese and sauce.

Put the tacos in an oven-proof dish large enough to hold them in a single layer, and bake in a preheated 400° oven for 3 to 4 minutes, until the cheese melts. Serve immediately.

Serving Suggestions:

✛ Just before eating, sprinkle on your preferred amount of chopped tomatoes, onions, sliced jalapeños, lettuce, and your favorite hot sauce. Guacamole is also an excellent side dish for Tostados Compuestas.

An early family portrait: (left to right) Matt Jr., sister Kathy (in front of him), mother Janie (seated), wife Estella, · sister Gloria, Matt Sr., and sister Sissy.

REMEMBERING EL RANCHO AND YESTERDAY

Estella Martínez

Estella is Matt Jr.'s wife.

When Matt and I were first married, I was not so sure how to handle myself around the Martinez family. Matt had been elected vice-president of the Austin Restaurant Association; and, as his new bride and a new member in the organization, I was excited about being invited to attend a restaurant association meeting at Hill's Café, on the outskirts of Austin.

We were all eating T-bone steaks, and I wanted to make a good impression. I was being very proper, using my knife and fork the correct way, when I glanced over at my father-in-law in the chair next to me. He had his steak in his hands and was ripping the meat off the bone with his teeth.

I quickly looked away and hoped I was invisible. I was embarrassed, but it didn't seem to bother anyone else. They just kept eating.

I stopped worrying about my table manners from that point on.

Sloppy Joes

Those of you with little rascals may already know that Sloppy Joes are the perfect bait for luring young ones into the house on summer days. They just can't stay away from this stuff. I guess I'm still a child at heart, because neither can I.

Makes 6 to 8 sandwiches

For the Meat:

1	pound ground beef
1	teaspoon salt
2	teaspoons ground cumin
1 1/2	teaspoons granulated garlic
1/2	teaspoon black pepper

1/4	cup finely chopped sweet white onion
3	tablespoons finely chopped celery
3	tablespoons finely chopped green bell pepper

For the Rest:

3	tablespoons flour
1	(8-ounce) can tomato sauce

1	tablespoon chili powder
6–8	hamburger buns

First, combine the meat ingredients in a 10-inch skillet. Sauté the meat over medium heat for 4 to 5 minutes, until thoroughly cooked.

When the meat is cooked, add the flour and continue to sauté for 2 to 3 minutes over medium heat. Add the tomato sauce and chili powder, and sauté for another 1 to 2 minutes.

In an oven, toast the buns to the desired crispness and load 'em up with the sloppy joes. Use mayonnaise or mustard, pickles, onions, or any other garnish that suits your own taste buds.

Optional:

◆ Instead of toasted buns, Sloppy Joes are also good wrapped in flour tortillas.

Matt's Competition Chili

Contrary to what many people think, chili con carne, or just plain chili, is not from Mexico. I do not know what role my family played in the inventing and perfecting of chili, but we had our fingers in the bowl.

Having researched the subject for years, there's no doubt in my mind that chili originated in San Antonio, where it made an impact as early as the 1700s. My mother's side of the family—her roots anyway—are firmly planted in San Antonio dating back many, many years.

At heart, I am a romantic, and so I do love the story of the Lady in Blue. Perhaps it is even true. I want to tell it first, and then I will tell you about the Chili Queens of San Antonio.

The Lady in Blue was a real woman, Sister Mary of Agreda, and she was said to be as mysterious as she was beautiful. Sometime in the 1600s, Sister Mary appeared before the Native American Indians in what is now the southwestern portion of the United States. Her presence there was most remarkable considering that Sister Mary never set foot outside Spain.

At 16, she had entered a convent in Castille. A few years later, she began to have strange spells; she would slip into trances, often for days, in which her body became as lifeless as a soggy burrito.

Each time she regained consciousness, Sister Mary told others that her spirit had flown out of her body and traveled to some place very far away, where she bided her time preaching Christianity to tribes of so-called savages.

The early missionaries who helped settle parts of Texas, New Mexico, and Arizona, also believed that la Dama de Azul, as they called her, must have walked among the Indians. Their stories of a holy woman in blue were just too vivid and consistent.

One padre, Father Alonso de Benavides, first heard about the Lady in Blue while running a mission where El Paso now stands. Members of the West Texas Jumanos, a tribe that had not yet seen the White Man, kept telling the padre incredible tales of a nun preaching Christianity. They said her cheeks were rosy and her eyes big. A soggy burrito, she was not.

And then the Tiguas of New Mexico (and still of El Paso), and the Caddos, far away in the Piney Woods of deep East Texas and Louisiana, spread their own stories of a Lady in Blue.

When Father Alonso returned to Spain, he heard stories of Sister Mary's out-of-body experiences. They sounded too eerily similar to those he had heard from the Indians.

Fascinated, the padre sought out Sister Mary. In detail, she described for him wilderness scenes of the Southwest, including descriptions of specific tribe members. The padre was flabbergasted; he knew she had to have gone there.

Father Alonso was not alone. Sister Mary convinced the King of Spain and other merry old souls. They believed that her spirit had made a few transcontinental round trips. Perhaps she ran out of frequent flyer miles, but after convincing priests and kings and merry men all in a row, the sister never flew away again.

Somewhere along her early journeys, Mary of Agreda jotted down a chili con carne recipe calling for venison or antelope meat (a wild musk hog, in a pinch), with onions and tomatoes.

None of the early Conquistadors from Spain and not one Native American Indian tribe is known to have included chili con carne in their recipes.

My romantic nature wishes to believe the story about la Dama de Azul.

But what I really believe is that the Chili Queens of San Antonio were most likely responsible for the dish.

The Chili Queens of San Antonio were Mexican wives and widows—entrepreneurs, really—who gained not only their nickname but their reputation selling their unique dishes to cowboys living in the surrounding areas or just passing through.

The Chili Queens would set up stands out in the open near a market, or they'd grab a street corner. The cowboys would come to town, and they had to have a bowl of that chili. In fact, the cowboys were the ones who first started calling it chili, because of all the peppers and spices in it.

There was nothing fancy about their chili. The Chili Queens used the spices they had—cumin, chile ancho, chili powder, salt, pepper—with chopped shank meat or whatever was available. They'd throw in onions, possibly tomatoes.

Some of today's chili aficionados cry out, "No! You can't put beans in chili!"

Well, back in the old days, when you were hungry, you put whatever the heck you had in the pot.

Here's my favorite recipe. It's been good to me. Now it can be good to you, too. I like the way the flavors blend so well into one.

Makes 18 to 20 servings

For the Broth:

- 3 tablespoons vegetable oil or other oil of your choice
- 2 stalks celery, coarsely chopped
- 2 cups coarsely chopped green bell pepper
- 3 cups coarsely chopped sweet white onions
- 1/2 cup coarsely chopped fresh cilantro
- 1 bay leaf
- 2 tablespoons crushed and finely chopped garlic
- 1 tablespoon salt
- 5 pounds beef soup bones
- 2 cups dry pinto beans
- 3 quarts water

For the Meat:

- 5 pounds round steak, trimmed and cut into 1/4-inch cubes
- 4 tablespoons reserved fat from the broth
- 3 tablespoons ground cumin
- 2 tablespoons granulated garlic
- 2 1/2 teaspoons black pepper
- 1 teaspoon white pepper
- 5 tablespoons chili powder
- 1 tablespoon dried leaf oregano

Finishing Ingredients:

- 1 (6-ounce) can tomato paste, or 3 (14-ounce) cans whole stewed tomatoes (optional)
- 2 teaspoons smooth peanut butter

  Salt, to taste
- 5 tablespoons cornstarch mixed with 1 cup water

  Chili powder, to taste

First, make the broth: Heat the oil in a large soup pot, and sauté the celery, bell pepper, onions, cilantro, bay leaves, garlic, and salt for 2 to 3 minutes, until the onions are translucent. Add the bones, beans, and water, and bring to a boil. Skim the residue from the top, reserving 4 tablespoons of fat for the meat. Lower the heat and simmer for 3 hours. When the broth has cooked, strain and discard all the solids. Refrigerate the broth.

Now comes the chili: Brown the beef lightly in the broth's reserved fat, 6 to 10 minutes. Add all of the seasonings and sauté for 2 to 3 minutes. Add the cold broth and bring it to a simmer. Cook uncovered until the meat is tender, approximately 1 to 1^1/$_2$ hours. Be extremely careful not to overcook it. Add more water as needed to maintain a nonpasty consistency.

If desired, when the meat is tender add the tomato paste or stewed tomatoes. Add the peanut butter, which is especially pertinent. Season with salt to taste. At the end of cooking, add the cornstarch mixture. Carefully drizzle in a little at a time until the chili reaches the desired consistency—pourable, without being runny and without having to scoop it out.

Continue to cook for 5 minutes more. Adjust the taste with chili powder and additional salt. Enjoy.

Matt's Big-Time Eatin' Chili

My favorite ingredients for this recipe, which is especially friendly to your body on a cold day, are the garlic, cumin, and chili powder (I prefer the McCormick Dark, if available).

Makes 2 to 4 servings

1	pound venison, trimmed and cut into 1/4-inch cubes, or ground beef or cubed beef
1	tablespoon chili powder
2	teaspoons ground cumin
1 1/2	teaspoons granulated garlic
1	teaspoon salt
1/2	teaspoon black pepper
1	tablespoon cornstarch

1/2	teaspoon dried leaf oregano
4	tablespoons coarsely chopped sweet white onion
3	tablespoons coarsely chopped red bell pepper
1	(14-ounce) can whole stewed tomatoes
2	cups water

Preferably using a black iron skillet or saucepan, brown the meat for 3 to 4 minutes, until it's slightly gray (no oil is necessary), then drain the fat. Add all the seasonings, the onion, and pepper, and sauté for 2 minutes.

Add the tomatoes and water, and simmer uncovered until tender, approximately 1 hour or more, until the meat reaches the desired tenderness (the longer you cook it, the more tender it gets; the choice is yours).

More water may be added if needed. Adjust the salt and chili powder to your taste. Serve right away.

Children's Chili

As that old country song cautions, Mamas might not want to let their babies grow up to be cowboys; but I've never known a mama who minded her child being a chili-head.

Chili-head children are known to make better grades in school, are more respectful to their elders, are more entertaining to guests, and grow up to be incredible parents.

Here's something a child can learn to make, with a little supervision from Mom and Dad. Who knows? This could be the first step toward your child's becoming a chili-head. Consider it a blessing, and thank me for this the very next time you see me.

Makes 4 to 6 servings

1	pound hamburger meat		1/2	teaspoon black pepper
1	tablespoon chili powder (McCormick Dark, if available)		1	tablespoon cornstarch
2	teaspoons ground cumin		1/4	cup ketchup
1/2	teaspoon granulated garlic		2 1/2	cups water
1	teaspoon salt		1/2	teaspoon smooth peanut butter

Lightly brown the meat until it loses its redness. Discard all the fat from the pan, then add all the dry ingredients. Sauté for 2 minutes, then add the ketchup, water, and peanut butter. Simmer for 20 minutes.

Estella Martinez

One day I was at El Rancho when in walked Joseph Cotten. I said to my father-in-law, Matt Sr., "Look, it's Joseph Cotten."

He said, "Who's Joseph Cotten?"

I said, "You know, the old movie actor."

Before I knew it, he was at Joseph Cotten's table, shaking hands, assuring him, "I've seen everything you've done. You are one of my all-time favorites."

My father-in-law had that knack for making customers feel good about themselves.

Matt Sr. (far left) with a few World War II military buddies.

Picadillos (The First Time I Ever Cooked for Others)

I was in the Boy Scouts one October years ago when I was still a pup, maybe 12 or 13 years old. Six or eight of us decided to do some camping on a nearby creek, and I was put in charge of the grub.

We weren't going outside the Austin city limits, but we were feeling pretty important because we were Boy Scouts on a mission, heading out on our own.

None of us had cooked, but at least I had lived in a few kitchens, especially Granny's, Mom's, and El Rancho's. Still, I was sorta nervous about my assignment, so I went to Granny Gaytan, whose kitchen had always been filled with smells that sometimes tickled the nose and sometimes caused the nose to have a mind of its own. These were aromas that can only come from God's gardens.

"Cold front's comin' in," Granny warned. "Might get cold as mischief. I'll give you something that ought to taste good and keep your bellies warm, too. Take extra blankets and build a nice fire.

"There'll be a full moon," she added, "and the sky will be clear."

Granny was right, it got really cold before the sun nodded off, which was early.

In the summertime, the ground where we used to camp is grassy and soft, but in the winter it's hard and dry. First thing we did was build a fire out of dry twigs. I wasn't supposed to cook until the next day, so we stood around the fire and talked a lot, sometimes about being Boy Scouts, sometimes about being ourselves. We shivered a lot, too.

Our feet got colder and colder, but I think every one of us was still happy to be there. It was almost midnight before we hushed up with all our talking and got around to realizing our bellies were already grumbling for a fillup.

Granny had given me a pound of hamburger meat, a can of peas, a can of corn, a can of whole tomatoes, 2 potatoes and 2 onions. She also gave me a little ol' pack of spices that included some garlic powder, ground cumin, salt and pepper, and some flour wrapped in wax paper.

We were so cold we couldn't even peel the potatoes. We didn't even wash them. We just threw 'em in the pot.

Granny had told me, "When you get there, go ahead and cut your potatoes, brown your meat, throw in your spices and everything else on top, and add a little water. You'll make your friends a very tasty picadillo."

Sure enough, we got everything cooked, and we sat around eating off our tin plates, and I think we had the best meal we've ever had our whole lives. I can still remember sopping up the gravy and juices with that Rainbo Bread. We sopped up every ounce of that stew.

We got our bellies good and full, huddled up a little longer, and then decided we'd had all the fun we could stand. So we headed for home. We were frozen, and our warm beds were calling.

After that night, everybody kept telling my parents and three sisters what a great cook I was. Among my friends, I became THE cook.

My granny told me, "If you can cook, you'll be welcomed any place you go."

Granny was always right.

Makes 4 to 6 servings (6 cups)

3 tablespoons oil of your choice	2 teaspoons granulated garlic
1 pound ground beef (or ground chicken, turkey, pork, venison, or elk; I recommend a pork/venison combination)	3/4 teaspoon dried oregano
	3 tablespoons flour
	4 cups water
1/2 cup coarsely chopped sweet white onion	1 (4-ounce) can tomato sauce
1/4 cup coarsely chopped celery	2 cups fresh or frozen corn kernels
1/4 cup coarsely chopped red or green bell pepper	2 cups fresh or frozen peas
1 1/2 teaspoons salt	1 large potato, quartered and sliced thin
3/4 teaspoon black pepper	Salt and black pepper, to taste
3 teaspoons ground cumin	

In a large skillet, heat the oil and lightly brown the meat 4 to 5 minutes, until it loses its redness and looks fully cooked. Tilt the pan and discard as much oil as possible. Return the

Matt Martinez's Culinary Frontier

meat to medium heat and add the onion, celery, bell pepper, and seasonings. Sauté for 2 to 3 minutes—don't worry if there's some sticking, but do not let the meat burn.

Add the water, tomato sauce, corn, peas, and potatoes. Bring the mixture to a light simmer and cook 8 to 10 minutes, until the potatoes flake with the touch of a fork. Adjust the seasoning with salt and pepper. Serve hot.

Optional:

♦ Any combination of thinly sliced carrots, mushrooms, zucchini, yellow squash, cabbage, and/or okra may be used instead of the peas and corn. But do not exceed 4 cups total vegetables, and add them just after the meat is browned.

♦ Cilantro lovers, add 3 tablespoons of chopped fresh cilantro while simmering the stew.

♦ Chili-heads, add 2 to 3 teaspoons of chili powder while simmering.

Crispy Tacos

There once lived in Austin a Mexican American who was so talented inside the boxing ring that he became known as "the Battling Newsboy."

While a young man in the late 1930s, when he wasn't throwing the Austin American-Statesman on his neighborhood route, the Battling Newsboy was boxing.

He was so good that he became the first Mexican-American Golden Gloves boxing champion from Austin. He had a wicked left hook, and a right hand of stone.

Records show that on his way to the lightweight Golden Gloves title, the Battling Newsboy won 110 of 113 amateur fights. He was 32–2 as a pro.

Along came World War II, prompting the Battling Newsboy to trade his paper route for Army fatigues in 1940. For three years, he served as a boxing instructor for the military—until being transferred to the South Pacific, where he was a gunnery sergeant the rest of the war.

When he returned to Austin, his surest way of making a buck was to fight any and all takers—with side bets encouraged, of course. And so the Battling Newsboy took his boxing into the bars around Austin and challenged all comers.

It got to where nobody with any common sense would fight the guy. He was so feared, in fact, that he and a small entourage of backers hit the road, to San Antonio and Houston and Dallas, where the Battling Newsboy picked up fights in bars for $1 to $5 a bet, sometimes

more. Often, one of his companions could be heard yelling above the din, "C'mon, finish this guy off, we've got to get to the next bar."

I know this story to be true, for the Battling Newsboy is my father, Matt Martinez, Sr.

His Austin restaurant, Matt's El Rancho, remains one of the city's busiest restaurants. And since 1952, when El Rancho first opened at its original location on First Street, my father's tacos have been a hit. Try them and see.

Matt Martinez, Sr., the boxer known as "the Battling Newsboy"

Makes 12 crispy tacos

For the Meat:

1   pound ground beef

1   teaspoon salt

2   teaspoons ground cumin

1 1/2   teaspoons granulated garlic

1/2   teaspoon black pepper

1/4   cup finely chopped sweet white onion

3   tablespoons finely chopped celery

3   tablespoons finely chopped green bell pepper

For the Rest:

12   taco shells

12   heaping teaspoons grated Monterey Jack or American cheese

2   tablespoons Ranchero or Tomatillo Salsa (pages 31 and 30)

First, combine the meat ingredients in a 10-inch skillet. Sauté the meat over medium heat for 4 to 5 minutes, until thoroughly cooked.

Warm your taco shells in an oven at low heat for 2 to 3 minutes. Fill and garnish your tacos with cheese and salsa. Eat immediately.

Serving Suggestions:

✤ For a taco party, place the meat on a hot platter or pan and allow your guests to fill up the shells as they desire.

✤ Chile con Queso (page 59) is good poured over the meat.

✤ The meat is also excellent rolled in flour tortillas.

✤ Remember to heat (and reheat) flour tortillas on a hot skillet, never in the oven or microwave.

Matts Jr. and Sr. near the bar of the old El Rancho on First Street in Austin

Janie Martinez

Janie was 15 years old when she met her husband-to-be, Matt, Sr. Matt was a 20-year-old tough guy, but Janie knew he had a heart of gold. They married about a year later, in 1944.

Before we married, Matt was a shadow. Everywhere I went, he wanted to go. He was just out of the service, and he had a job as a waiter at a nice restaurant in Austin. One day he said to me, "I want to marry you, and I want us to open our own restaurant. I'm tired of working for others; from now on, just myself. You know how to cook?"

I was surprised. I said to him, "Only like my mother and grandmother cook."

He nodded and said, "Okay."

I could not imagine. I said, "Matt, how are we going to open a restaurant? We have no money."

He said, "I have pulled together $75, and I know how we can borrow $300 more. If we can sell just $50 a day in food, we'll be fine."

Each day, our lunch plate included four basic items besides Mexican food: Chicken and dumplings, fried chicken, roast beef, and ribs. Everything sold. We kept adding a few recipes and cutting back a few when necessary. Each year for four years, we built another dining room to the house that was our original restaurant on East First. We just kept growing.

Flautas

In Spanish, flauta *means "flute."*

    Flautas are tightly rolled corn tortillas with an assortment of fillings. Some fast-food restaurants mistakenly call them "taquitas," which are actually old-fashioned tacos.

Makes 6 servings (4 flautas per person as a main course)

1	cup oil of your choice
24	corn tortillas
1 1/2–2	cups filling of your choice (shredded beef, ground beef, chicken, beans, or cheese)

In a skillet or pan, heat the oil to hot. With tongs, dip the tortillas in the oil on both sides to moisten them, no more than a second or 2, and stack them.

    Place about 1 tablespoon of the filling in the center of a tortilla and spread it out lengthwise. Roll the tortilla tightly, and repeat the process until all are filled and rolled.

    Reserve just enough oil in the skillet to keep its bottom moist. Add a few flautas at a time, keeping the tortillas seam side down. Cook them 5 to 10 seconds, then gently roll them in the skillet until they are golden brown on all sides. Serve.

Serving Suggestions:

  ✦ Serve flautas with hot sauce, Traditional Guacamole (page 62), Chile con Queso (page 59), Ranchero Salsa (page 31), or Tomatillo Salsa (page 30).

  ✦ Sour cream is also an ideal accompaniment.

Matt Martínez, Jr.

When I was maybe eight years old, I went to work doing whatever I could at the family restaurant. I was a little shy, but I was ready to earn my keep.

Before long, I was cleaning tables, washing dishes, storing stuff. I thought it was great. Nobody messed with you, and you got to get all dirty.

It was from washing dishes that I began to learn how to coordinate a game plan so that I could handle the load when customers kept walking through the front door and the dishes kept piling up around me.

Before things got too crazy, I would glance up from the sink and look at the counter where the cooks placed the prepared plates. I wanted to know what kinds of plates and bowls were going out. I'd line up more big plates or more mugs or clean more silverware, based on what I judged the needs to be at the time.

Then I was moved into the actual kitchen area and put in charge of salads. Waiters would come in yelling orders in six or seven voices and dialects, and somehow the cooks could remember each one. I was amazed. I doubt I could do it today. I don't know how we did it then.

Pretty soon, I was handling the dish-out, where you've got to remember even more. During the *really busy* hours, the waiters would come in and attach the orders to a hanging wire. Half the waiters couldn't write, so you had to learn each of their scratch systems.

For some, if they marked an "X" on an order, that meant enchiladas. Others used the "X" for tacos or something else. You just learned them.

I'm not sure, but somewhere in this story, there must be one about life as well.

Matt Jr.'s Uncle Mack (left), selling tamales in Austin with a couple of his girl friends.

Smoked Brisket

The great thing about making a brisket is that there are so many ways to use the leftovers by shredding or mixing it with other items to make several more full meals.

Makes 8 to 12 servings

8–12   pounds beef brisket (Short, fat briskets with a thick covering of fat have the best flavor. Never use a trimmed brisket.)

Texas Sprinkle (page 42, optional)

Matt's Simple Barbecue Sauce (page 38)

For Barbecuing:

Hickory, pecan, or oak wood chips, soaked in water for 1 hour; charcoal briquettes or hard-wood charcoal; a charcoal grill and a conventional oven.

Season the untrimmed brisket, if desired, with the Texas Sprinkle. Light the charcoal in the grill and allow it to cook down until the charcoal is ash white. When the charcoal has reached the proper temperature, place a cup of soaked wood chips on the coals.

Grill the brisket until dark and crusty on both sides, 30 to 40 minutes, turning it occasionally. Expect some flare-ups, but allow the meat to char.

Heat the oven to 200°. When the brisket is charred, place it on a rack, or in a roasting pan with a lid, or cover it with foil. Roast it for 1 hour per pound.

When the brisket is done, trim the fat and slice it thin across the grain. Serve it with Matt's Simple Barbecue Sauce.

If you're looking for more bang from your meat, use the Horseradish Sauce (page 39) as well. The recipe makes $^1/_2$ cup, enough to use on 4 meaty sandwiches.

How to Use Left-over Brisket:

+ Use it instead of ham to flavor beans or peas.
+ Add it to Chile con Queso (page 59) with cubed avocados.
+ Add it to split pea soup instead of ham.
+ Fold it into an omelet.
+ Use it in Oriental-style fried rice or Cajun-style dirty rice.
+ Sauté it with onions and chile peppers for scrambled eggs.
+ Use it to fill flautas, tacos, burritos, or enchiladas.
+ Use it to top Mexican pizza.
+ Add it to marinara sauce for spaghetti.
+ Make a brisket salad instead of chicken salad.
+ Simmer it with bottled salsa for an easy Huevos Rancheros sauce (page 11).
+ Use it to fill a flour tortilla, top it with queso, and roll it up.

Brisket (with Smoked Bob)

Bob Armstrong's only claim to fame is that I named a dip after him.

Many years ago, I was in the kitchen working 90 to nuthin' in charge of salads and appetizers. Because I was the owner's teen-age son, all the other employees liked to watch me run out of stuff or get confused. I really had to stay on my toes, which meant being prepared for anything.

One day, in walked Bob Armstrong, a longtime politician who had been Land Commissioner of Texas. Mr. Armstrong just walked into the kitchen anytime he got a wild hair.

"Little Matt," he said, "gimme something different for an appetizer. Something not on the menu."

I said, "Go sit down, it's on the way."

I grabbed whatever jumped into my hands. I threw some taco meat in the bottom of a bowl, then I threw in guacamole and sour cream, and then I made some chile con queso and threw it all in the oven.

The waitress later told me when she took it out to him, Mr. Armstrong muttered, "That ain't nothing but a bowl of queso."

Then he stuck his spoon in there and he saw guacamole, sour cream, and some beef. The waitress says he hushed up for a while and started eating, and then his eyes got as big around as saucers. I guess it worked.

I had the next day off and went fishing. People kept going into El Rancho and ordering "that Bob Armstrong dip that's not on the menu," but nobody at the restaurant had any idea what the clamor was all about. I got in trouble and wasn't even there.

What we didn't realize is that Mr. Armstrong had gone back to the state Capitol building after lunch that day and told everybody about this amazing appetizer he'd had.

When I went to work the following day, the orders kept coming in. I barely remembered the recipe because I simply had been throwing whatever was nearby into the pot.

Today, Smoked Bob is a smoked, shredded brisket or tenderloin served with queso, guacamole, sour cream, and onions. It's one of our most popular appetizers, and many people also order it when they want a lighter meal.

Smoked Bob wasn't even on any of our menus until the spring of '96 when we added it to the No Place menu in Dallas.

Makes 4 to 6 servings as a main course (6 to 8 as an appetizer)

1 batch Chile con Queso (page 59)	1 cup sour cream
4 cups shredded Smoked Brisket (see preceding recipe)	12–16 flour tortillas
Traditional Guacamole (page 62) made from 2 avocados	Slices of green onion and jalapeño, as a garnish

Prepare the queso and pour some on a warm plate. Lop on the shredded brisket over the queso in the middle of the plate, and lop on some guacamole and sour cream over the queso on the sides. Serve with the tortillas and mix tastes to your heart's desire.

Serving Suggestions:

✚ Use the tortillas to sop up the queso, or to fill with the brisket, guacamole, sour cream, and queso.

✚ Besides green onion and jalapeño, hot sauce also goes good with Smoked Bob.

King Ranch Beef Casserole

In October 1994, I was invited on the Oprah Winfrey show to discuss the health aspects of Mexican food. Let me tell you, the entire process of putting on a talk show, with all of those commercial breaks timed to the second, was a recipe all its own.

As for being health-wise, I side with those who say it's always best not to overindulge in anything. And yet, I also feel we've become way too paranoid about everything we eat.

If you give your body enough exercise and don't go on binges every day, why not an occasional treat? That's what this book is all about—those times you want to treat yourself.

My family has always been health conscious. My mother and her mother served everything fresh from the garden. They did not like to use a lot of grease or fat, and they influenced me to look out for stuff that was overly greasy.

Not long ago, the American Heart Association and the Texas Beef Council asked me to take a dish known as the King Ranch Casserole, which normally included chicken and high fat, and to lighten it up but still substitute lean beef for the chicken. We served this King Ranch Beef Casserole at HeartFest, a week-long event the AHA sponsored in Austin.

This recipe has 312 calories and 6 grams of fat per serving, compared to 505 calories and 27 grams of fat in the original recipe.

Makes 6 to 8 servings

2 pounds beef sirloin

2 cups water

1 cup finely chopped sweet white onions

1/2 cup coarsely chopped red bell pepper

1/2 cup coarsely chopped green bell pepper

2–4 tablespoons coarsely chopped jalapeño

1 teaspoon salt

1 teaspoon black pepper

1 teaspoon ground cumin

1 teaspoon granulated garlic

1 tablespoon chili powder

1 (10-ounce) can diced green chile peppers and tomatoes

1 (16-ounce) can Beef Broth (or see page 48)

2/3 cup skim milk

8 ounces fat-free Cheddar cheese, shredded

12 corn tortillas

Put the beef and water in a pan and cook over low heat for 30 to 45 minutes, until the meat is fork-tender and cooked well enough to shred. Shred it by pulling the meat apart with 2 forks. Then set it aside. Preheat the oven to 350°.

In a large skillet without oil, sauté the onions and peppers with the seasonings for 2 to 3 minutes, until the onions are translucent.

Add the canned chiles and tomatoes, the beef broth, and milk, and simmer for 2 to 3 minutes. Stir in the cheese until it's melted. Add the cooked, shredded beef.

Quarter the tortillas and add them to the mixture. Pour everything into a casserole dish (nonstick cooking spray helps), and bake for 30 minutes.

Matt Martinez, Jr.

My father was always leery of being robbed. One of his tactics was to use my mother as a decoy. At closing time, he would give her all of the nickels, dimes, and pennies out of the cash register, placing them in a bag, while he rolled up all of the bills in a big wad and stuffed them into his pants pockets.

One day, my mother was getting into her car with the bag of chump change when two guys with guns popped up from the back

Matt Sr. switched from Falstaff to Budweiser the day the Clydesdales came to Austin in 1953. Notice little Matt at the bottom left, just over the parked car's headlight.

seat. They were less than pleased when they discovered she had so little money. And so, they kidnaped her.

They drove Mom to a bad, secluded part of East Austin and argued about whether to kill her and dump her body out there. She pleaded, telling them, "I have babies at home who need me. Please, do not kill me."

They dropped Mom off in the middle of nowhere and drove away in her car.

Dad, meanwhile, was expecting her. He thought she was just going outside to put the bag in the car. When she didn't return, he figured Mom must have got mad at him about something. He helped himself to another Falstaff beer and went home.

Mom was walking down the road, weeping, when one of our El Rancho customers happened by. He picked her up and took her home.

The moral of this story?

It pays to be nice to your customers. Maybe they'll remember you when you need them most.

Early Texas Chicken-Fried Steak

The likelihood of meeting a native-born Texan from my generation who has never downed a chicken-fried steak borders on the impossible. Any such person belongs in Ripley's Believe It or Not.

If you can perfect the making of this particular chicken-fried recipe—and I know you can—it'll pay dividends as you try your hand at the variations that follow.

Makes 4 to 6 servings

For the Meat:

1–1 1/2 pounds of one of the following meats, ground beef or fillets (fillets must be pounded out to 3/4 inches); beef round or flank steak; elk sirloin; venison tenderloin; or any ground meat such as turkey, emu, or wild game

1 heaping tablespoon chopped onion, celery, or mushrooms (optional)

1 heaping tablespoon cracker meal or bread crumbs (optional)

1 egg white

For the Coating:

1 cup flour

1 teaspoon salt

1/2 teaspoon black pepper

2 eggs

1/2 cup milk (if using buttermilk, use 1 cup and eliminate the eggs)

To Fry and Serve:

Oil or shortening of your choice: lard, bacon drippings, Crisco, corn or vegetable oil

Perfect Cream Gravy (page 43) or Matt's Lighter Gravy (page 44)

To prepare the meat: If using very lean ground meat (such as elk, venison, emu, or ground eye of round), combine it with the chopped vegetables, the meal or bread crumbs, and one (or less) egg white. If using another ground meat, mix it with 1 egg white only and eliminate the vegetables and meal or crumbs.

Using $1/4$ pound of meat per serving, cut the steaks $1/2$ inch thick and trim them of fat. Pound them with a meat tenderizer or the back of a knife, taking care not to tear the meat. Ground meats should be formed into patties, which will be treated like tenderized steaks.

To make the coating: Combine the dry ingredients in a mixing bowl. In a saucepot, combine the eggs and milk and heat lightly. Dredge the meat in the flour mixture, then in the milk, then again in the flour. Fry the steaks in $1/8$ inch of the oil or shortening of your choice on medium-high heat until they're golden brown. The steaks should be well done but not dry. This should take from $2^1/2$ to 3 minutes per side, depending on the meat you are using.

Drain the steaks on paper towels and keep them warm in a low oven while you make the gravy.

Variation:

◆ After dredging the steaks in the coating mixture, dredge them in cracker meal or bread crumbs for a second coating. This will give you a different texture. Cracker meal will make the coating crispier. Bread crumbs will have a rougher texture, for a different feel in the mouth.

Chicken-Fried Steak Tampiquena

Steak tampiquena is a steak smothered in onions, peppers, and salsa. One batch of my Ranchero Salsa covers all of those bases.

Makes 4 servings

- 4 cooked Early Texas Chicken-Fried Steaks (see preceding recipe)
- 1 batch Ranchero Salsa (page 31)

- 4 teaspoons sour cream
- 4 heaping tablespoons shredded Monterey Jack cheese

Preheat the oven to 375°. Prepare the steaks and the salsa, and place the steaks on a large baking platter. Smother the steaks in the salsa, and over each steak spread 1 teaspoon of sour cream and 1 tablespoon of cheese.

Bake the steaks for 3 to 4 minutes, until the cheese is bubbling. Serve immediately.

Serving Suggestions:
- ✦ Serve with steamed rice or buttered pasta.
- ✦ Beans and rice are good with this dish.

Chicken-Fried Steak in Tomatillo Sauce

This has been among our biggest sellers at the Y.O. Ranch Restaurant, in the West End Historic District of downtown Dallas.

Makes 4 servings

- 4 cooked Early Texas Chicken-Fried Steaks (see page 152)
- 1 batch Tomatillo Salsa (page 30)
- 4 teaspoons sour cream
- 4 heaping tablespoons shredded Monterey Jack cheese

Preheat the oven to 375°. Prepare the steaks and the salsa, and place the steaks on a large baking platter. Smother the steaks in the salsa, and over each steak spread 1 teaspoon of sour cream and 1 tablespoon of cheese.

Bake the steaks for 3 to 4 minutes, until the cheese is bubbling. Serve right away.

Serving Suggestions:
- ✦ Serve with steamed rice or buttered pasta.
- ✦ Beans and rice are good with this dish.

Julia Child had her first chicken-fried steak at Matt's No Place in November 1993. Having thoroughly enjoyed the experience, she dubbed Matt Jr.'s cooking style "the common man's culinary frontier," and reported to the Dallas Morning News, "I ate so much I hurt myself."

Cowboy-Style Chicken-Fried Steak

Cowboys were known to fire up their bellies with many kinds of peppers. This steak works quite nicely in that regard.

Makes 4 servings

- 4 cooked Early Texas Chicken-Fried Steaks (page 152)
- 1 batch Matt's Big-Time Eatin' Chili (page 132)
- 4 teaspoons finely chopped sweet white onion
- 4 tablespoons shredded American cheese

Preheat the oven to 375°. Prepare the steaks and the chili, and place the steaks on a large baking platter. Smother the steaks in the chili, and over each steak spread 1 teaspoon of onion and 1 tablespoon of cheese.

Bake the steaks for 3 to 4 minutes, until the cheese is bubbling. Serve immediately.

Chile Rellenos (The Love of LBJ and Lady Bird Johnson)

From his early days of Texas politicking to being Senate Majority Leader, Vice-President, and President of the United States, Lyndon Johnson and wife Lady Bird ate my family's chile rellenos, enchiladas, tacos, rice, and beans.

Lyndon was a big man. He ate like a big man.

Lady Bird is not a big woman. But she has a big heart, and she sure did like my family's cooking.

Each time LBJ and Lady Bird flew in or out of Austin's Bergstrom Air Force Base, they dropped by Matt's El Rancho for a quick fix that could satisfy them all day long.

My family also catered many of the parties that LBJ and Lady Bird threw at their LBJ Ranch in Johnson City, in the Hill Country outside of Austin.

I was a shy lad the first time I remember seeing them. I was in the kitchen one day at the original El Rancho on East First Street when a fleet of limousines wheeled up. The secret service men came rushing through the back door, and I was scared half to death.

By then, I was accustomed to crowds, but I wasn't prepared for anything like this. The first El Rancho was next door to a plumbing company whose primary form of advertisement was a commode lid hanging from a tree out front. Flashy scenes and limousines were not common neighborhood occurrences.

The secret service positioned themselves in each corner of the restaurant, and in walked this large man with twinkling eyes.

I was so scared I ran behind the counter and hid beneath the cash register, near the candy and pralines.

Over time, I began to relax and understand the ritual. The secret service would cordon off the block, then come in and look at me and say in a real important tone, "Hey, Little Matt, we're here!"

Then, they'd take their positions, and LBJ and Lady Bird would walk right in the back door, go through the kitchen, sit down, and order up a plate of chile rellenos, or cheese enchiladas, with beans, rice, and a taco.

Sometimes when he got finished, Lyndon would come up to me and say, "Hi, Little Matt," and his big mitt of a hand would swallow up my little fingers.

LBJ was an absolute charmer, with the softest eyes and the warmest smile. He really did melt away my fears.

In 1993, I was in Austin attending a function at El Rancho, when I felt a small hand on one of mine.

"Little Matt, how are you?" It was Lady Bird, as elegant and charming as ever. I was flattered. After all these years, she had not forgotten.

Lady Bird and LBJ never complained when we catered for them. Well, Lyndon did once announce to his guests, "I realize some of you might have got some cold food . . . that's not typical of these folks."

And with that, he went on with his visiting.

Lyndon loved basic Tex-Mex. He had a real soft spot for our chile rellenos.

Today, chile rellenos are probably the most popular item on the menu at Matt's El Rancho. Originally, chile rellenos were made with egg whites, which held too much fat, and chile anchos, which dominated the other tastes. My mother perfected this recipe long ago.

Makes 6 to 8 chile rellenos (3 or 4 servings)

For the Meat:

- 1 pound ground beef
- 1 teaspoon salt
- 2 teaspoons ground cumin
- 1 1/2 teaspoons granulated garlic
- 1/2 teaspoon black pepper
- 1/4 cup finely chopped sweet white onion
- 3 tablespoons finely chopped celery
- 3 tablespoons finely chopped bell pepper

For the Rest:

- 1 batch Ranchero Salsa (page 31)
  Oil for frying
- 6 fresh Anaheim peppers
- 2 cups flour
- 1/2 teaspoon salt
- 1/4 teaspoon black pepper
- 2 cups buttermilk
- 2 cups grated American cheese
- 1/4 cup raisins
- 1/4 cup chopped pecans

To prepare the meat: Combine the ingredients in a 10-inch skillet. Sauté the meat over medium heat for 4 to 5 minutes, until thoroughly cooked.

Prepare the salsa. Preheat the oven to 375°.

Completely wipe down and dry the Anaheim peppers. In a skillet, heat oil to a depth of 3/4 to 1 inch to 375°. Roll the whole peppers around in the hot oil for 1 to 1 1/2 minutes, causing them to blister. Remove the peppers, wrap them in a damp cloth, and let them sit for 5 to 10 minutes. Then, remove the pepper skins, split each pepper, seed, and remove all the membranes.

In a bowl, mix the flour, salt, and black pepper. Dust the peppers in the flour mixture, roll them in the buttermilk, and dust each again in the flour. Fry the peppers in the oil over moderate heat until the batter is golden brown.

Arrange the fried peppers in an oven-proof dish. Divide the meat evenly over the tops of the peppers, then sprinkle with the cheese. Bake for 4 to 5 minutes, until the cheese starts to melt. While the dish is still in the oven, add the raisins and pecans, and continue baking for 1 or 2 minutes, until the cheese starts to bubble. Serve immediately.

Optional:

- ◆ You may use peppers other than Anaheim, but if they are too hot they take away from the overall taste.
- ◆ Tomatillo Salsa (page 30) may be substituted for the Ranchero Salsa.

Early Texas (Poor-Boy) Enchiladas

This is the granddaddy of all enchiladas, the way they were made before anybody had ever heard of chili.

They were originally made with goat cheese, farmer's cheese, any cheese you could get your hands on.

Makes 2 to 4 servings (8 enchiladas)

1 batch Poor-Boy Enchilada Sauce (page 50)	2 cups shredded Longhorn Cheddar or American cheese
1 cup vegetable oil	1 cup finely chopped sweet white onions
8 corn tortillas	

Preheat the oven to 350°. After you've made the sauce, heat the oil in a skillet on medium heat. With tongs, carefully swipe each tortilla through the grease, no more than 2 seconds. Drag the tortilla over the side of the skillet, removing the excess grease, and stack the tortillas on a warm plate. One by one, dip the tortillas into the salsa and stack them again on the plate.

Fill the center of all 8 tortillas with some of the cheese and onions, reserving some cheese for topping. Spread the fillings from end to end, then tightly roll up each tortilla.

Arrange the enchiladas in a 12-inch oven-proof dish. Spread the rest of the salsa over the tortillas, and sprinkle more cheese on top. Bake the enchiladas for 10 to 15 minutes, until the cheese is completely melted. Serve immediately.

Texas Enchiladas (Chili, Cheese, and Onion)

These are the most popular enchiladas in Texas today. Our restaurants have sold millions.

Makes 4 servings (8 enchiladas)

- 1 batch Matt's Big-Time Eatin' Chili (page 132)
- 1 cup vegetable oil
- 8 corn tortillas

- 2 cups shredded Longhorn Cheddar, Monterey Jack, or American cheese
- 1 cup finely chopped onions

After you've made the chili, preheat the oven to 350°. Heat the oil in a skillet on medium heat. With tongs, carefully swipe each tortilla through the grease, no more than 2 seconds. Drag the tortilla over the side of the skillet, removing the excess grease, and stack the tortillas on a warm plate. One by one, dip the tortillas into the chili and stack them again on the plate.

Fill the center of all 8 tortillas with some of the cheese and onions. Spread the fillings from end to end, then tightly roll up each tortilla.

Arrange the enchiladas in a 12-inch oven-proof dish. Spread the rest of the chili over the tortillas, and sprinkle more cheese on top. Bake the enchiladas for 10 to 15 minutes, until the cheese is completely melted. Serve right away.

REMEMBERING EL RANCHO AND YESTERDAY

John Anders

A Dallas Morning News humor columnist for three decades, John, in a previous life, was student assistant to Jones Ramsey in the University of Texas Sports Information Office.

Matt Senior once told me that Jones Ramsey holds the record for most consecutive meals at El Rancho. He says Jones ate every meal there for nine consecutive days.

 The restaurant was closed one day a week. Legend has it that on that day, Jones packed a sack lunch before going to work, then at noon drove over to the El Rancho parking lot and sat out in his car and ate.

Bill Morgan

Bill was Sports Information Director of the Southwest Conference from 1968 to 1987.

Nine straight days? For Ramsey? Is that all? He ought to be ashamed, if that's the best he ever did. Knowing Jones's love of the place, that record should have fallen some time in the mid-to-late '60s.

Jones Ramsey

Actually, it was fifteen days in a row. At least once, sometimes twice a day.

But that's because of the sportswriters. They wouldn't let me take them anywhere else.

Darrell Royal

Fifteen in a row? That's a pretty good record.

I could eat Tex-Mex fifteen days in a row, if you cover breakfast. I'd want Lupe waiting on me. She's done it all these years. She knows I want it all at the same time—the stuffed jalapeños with some beef on 'em, at the same time I have my main course.

Chicken Enchiladas with Tomatillo Salsa

Green enchiladas really woke up a new generation of Mexican food eaters. The tomatillo sauce started catching on in the mid-1950s and keeps getting more popular. Magic things happen with this mixture of tastes.

Makes 4 servings (8 enchiladas)

1 batch Tomatillo Salsa (page 30)	2 cups grated Monterey Jack cheese, loosely packed
1 cup vegetable oil	1 tablespoon freshly grated Parmesan cheese (optional)
8 corn tortillas	
8 tablespoons sour cream	
2 cups shredded cooked chicken (grilled, barbecued, or poached)	

After you've made the salsa, preheat the oven to 350°. Heat the oil in a skillet on medium heat. With tongs, carefully swipe each tortilla through the grease, no more than 2 seconds. Drag the tortilla over the side of the skillet, removing the excess grease, and stack the tortillas on a warm plate. One by one, dip the tortillas into the salsa and stack them again on the plate.

First, fill the center of each tortilla with 1 tablespoon of the sour cream, spreading it evenly along the center. Divide the chicken evenly, spreading it from end to end, then tightly roll up each tortilla.

Arrange the enchiladas in a 12-inch oven-proof dish. Spread the rest of the salsa over the rolled-up tortillas, and sprinkle on some cheese.

Bake the enchiladas for 10 to 15 minutes, until the cheese is completely melted. If using, sprinkle the Parmesan on top just before serving.

Optional:
◆ After baking, a little more sour cream on top won't hurt a thing.

Quesadillas (with Flour Tortillas)

Quesadillas are served with soups and salads, or as a complete meal with guacamole, hot sauce, and sour cream. The making of quesadillas requires an open mind, because you get to choose what you want to put in them.

My suggestions for fillers: Simple Chorizo (page 32); taco meat (see the meat portion of the Crispy Tacos recipe, page 139); cooked shredded beef, chicken, or pork; beans; Pico de Gallo (page 46); and/or, fresh spinach (it's great; see page 118).

Makes 4 to 6 servings

- 12 (5- or 6-inch) flour tortillas
- 12 heaping tablespoons grated Monterey Jack or American cheese
- 12 heaping tablespoons filler of your choice (see headnote for ideas)

Heat the flour tortillas for 1 or 2 minutes on each side in a medium hot skillet, until they are soft. Stack the tortillas.

When the tortillas are cool enough to handle but still very warm, spread 1 tablespoon of the cheese and filler of your choice evenly over half a tortilla and fold it in half. Continue until all the tortillas are filled.

Bring the pan back to medium heat. Place the quesadillas in the skillet and cook them for $1^1/_2$ to 2 minutes per side, until the cheese melts. Serve them warm.

Quesadillas (with Corn Tortillas)

Most quesadillas you get in restaurants today are made with flour tortillas. But I actually prefer them this way, with corn tortillas.

Use the same fillers as for the preceding Quesadillas with Flour Tortillas.

Makes 4 to 6 servings

1/2   cup oil of your choice

12   corn tortillas

12   heaping tablespoons grated
      Monterey Jack or American
      cheese

12   heaping tablespoons filler of your
      choice (see headnote, preceding
      recipe)

Heat the oil almost to smoking in a 10-inch skillet. With tongs, moisten the corn tortillas in the oil on both sides, stacking them as you remove them.

When cool enough to handle but still very warm, spread 1 tablespoon of the cheese and the filler of your choice evenly over half of each tortilla and fold them in half.

Without adding more oil, bring the pan back to medium heat. Place the quesadillas in the skillet, and cook them for 1 1/2 to 2 minutes per side, until the cheese melts. Serve them warm.

Serving Suggestions:

✦ Serve quesadillas as a complete meal with your favorite guacamole, hot sauce, and sour cream.

✦ Serve these as an appetizer with salads and soups.

Fideo (Vermicelli as a Main Dish)

This is a potent main dish that goes great with beans, tortillas (for dipping and sopping), and hot sauce.

Makes 4 to 6 servings

6 tablespoons vegetable oil or other oil of your choice	1/2 cup coarsely chopped green or red bell pepper
1 pound ground or cubed beef, pork, or venison	1/4 cup water, or Chicken or Beef Broth (canned, or see pages 47 and 48)
1 (5-ounce) box vermicelli	1/2 cup tomato sauce
1/2 teaspoon black pepper	Salt and additional pepper, to taste
1 1/2 teaspoons granulated garlic	
2 teaspoons ground cumin	
1 cup coarsely chopped white onions	

Using only half (3 tablespoons) the oil, sear the meat in a skillet for 3 to 4 minutes. When the meat is seared, tilt the skillet and drain off most of the excess oil. Remove the meat from the pan and set it aside.

In a separate skillet, heat the remaining 3 tablespoons of oil. Add the vermicelli, seasonings, and vegetables, and sauté, stirring constantly on medium heat, for 4 to 5 minutes, until the vermicelli is golden brown. Add the water or broth, the tomato sauce, and the seared meat.

Simmer on low heat for 7 to 8 minutes, until the vermicelli is "bitey"—tender, yet still firm. Adjust the seasoning with salt and pepper. Serve immediately.

Liver and Onions

Slightly taboo nowadays, Liver and Onions remains a classic meal for the old southern and southwestern buckaroos—and for the iron-deficient, as well. Sliced chicken or fully cooked turkey liver is an excellent substitute.

Makes 4 servings

4 slices of bacon	1–1 1/2 cups sliced sweet white onions
1/4 cup flour	2 pickled jalapeños, sliced
3/4 teaspoon salt, plus extra, to taste	1/2 cup water or Beef Broth (canned, or see page 48—optional)
1/4 teaspoon black pepper, plus extra, to taste	1 tablespoon brandy or bourbon (optional)
1 pound beef or calves liver, thinly sliced	

Fry the bacon on medium heat until crisp. Remove the bacon from the pan, crumble it up, and set it aside. In a bowl, combine the flour, 3/4 teaspoon salt, and 1/4 teaspoon pepper. Dust the liver in the seasoned flour, then sauté it in the bacon drippings for 3 1/2 to 4 minutes, until medium rare. Remove the liver from the skillet, and place it on a platter in a 180° oven while you make the gravy.

Remove all but 2 tablespoons of the bacon drippings from the skillet. Add the sliced onions and sauté for 2 to 3 minutes, until they are lightly browned.

Add the jalapeños, and continue cooking for one minute. Make a lighter gravy, if you want, by adding the water or broth, as well as the brandy or bourbon, to the oil left in the pan and cooking the gravy on low heat for 2 to 3 minutes, continually scraping the pan.

Adjust the seasoning with more salt and pepper, and spoon the gravy over the warm liver. Sprinkle the crumbled bacon on top and serve.

Serving Suggestion:

+ Serve Liver and Onions over buttered noodles or steamed rice.

Cabrito (Broiled Baby Goat)

Goat should be crispy on the outside, soft and tender on the inside. It may be served cubed or shredded. This simple barbecuing technique also works wonders with ribs and chicken.

Half the goat's weight is bone, so don't be misled by the seemingly gigantic servings.
Makes 4 to 6 servings

6–8   pounds baby goat, on the bone

For Washing:

2   gallons water

2   tablespoons salt

1   cup distilled white vinegar

For Basting:

2   tablespoons lard

1   tablespoon salt

2   cups warm water

To wash the goat: Pour the water into a large tub, and add the salt and vinegar. Place the meat in the tub and wash it thoroughly. While soaking the goat, build a large mesquite wood fire on the ground or in a barrel barbecue pit. The grate's cooking surface should be at least 24 by 36 inches. Burn the wood down to white coals, and make a 2- to 3-inch bed of coals under the grate by shoveling in the necessary amount of coals. Place the goat, whole or cut into pieces, on the grate, roughly 20 to 24 inches above the coals.

For the basting mixture: Add the lard and salt to the warm water and let them dissolve. Roast the goat for 2 to 3 hours, turning it frequently and applying the basting mixture, until the goat is golden brown on all sides.

Serving Suggestions:
✚ Side dishes for cabrito include beans, Spanish Rice (page 102), Traditional Guacamole (page 62), Pico de Gallo (page 46), tortillas, and lots of cold beer (Lone Star if available).

Carne Gasado with Bone

Experimentation is what turns cooking into your own art form. Instead of chicken, try substituting 3 pounds of beef or pork ribs (baby-backs are great), or 3 small squirrels, or 1 fryer armadillo, or 2 cottontails. But if you do substitute, plan on it taking 1¹/₂ to 2 hours to get the meat tender.

Makes 2 to 4 servings

- 3 pounds (approximately) whole chicken or parts (wings and breasts are best)
- ¹/₄ cup oil of your choice
- 4 tablespoons flour
- 1¹/₂ teaspoons salt
- 3 teaspoons ground cumin
- ³/₄ teaspoon black pepper
- 2 teaspoons granulated garlic
- 1 cup coarsely chopped sweet white onions
- ¹/₂ cup coarsely chopped red or green bell pepper
- ¹/₂ cup coarsely chopped celery
- 2 cups water, or Chicken or Beef Broth (canned, or see pages 47 and 48)
- 1 (14-ounce) can whole peeled and seeded tomatoes, with juice
- 1 (8-ounce) can tomato sauce

Trim the fat from the chicken. Heat the oil in a skillet and brown the chicken over medium high heat for 6 to 8 minutes, until the skin's golden on all sides. Remove the chicken from the pan and reserve it. Discard all but 3 tablespoons of the oil. Combine the flour and seasonings and lightly brown them in the remaining oil.

Add the chopped vegetables to the same pan and sauté them for 1 minute, or until the onions are translucent. Return the chicken to the pan, along with the water, tomatoes, and tomato sauce, and simmer uncovered on low heat for 1 hour, taking care that the chicken does not stick to the bottom of the pan. While simmering, occasionally spoon out the floating fat. Serve hot.

Serving Suggestions:
+ Serve Carne Gasado over pasta or the rice of your choice.
+ Sop up the juices with flour tortillas, corn tortillas, or coarse white bread.
+ Serve beans as a side dish.

Few people realize the Martinez family composed the first
Budweiser All-Women's Team.

The Perfect Steak

Telling a man or woman how to cook a steak is like telling someone how to make love on his or her honeymoon.

There was a time when most people I knew preferred their steaks medium well, or even well done. Today, medium-rare is the most popular request at Matt's No Place; and more people are ordering their steaks rare, especially rib-eyes and tenderloins.

Trial and error is the only way you're going to make steak to your liking; but, if you want to eliminate a few mistakes along the way, kindly ponder these general, "stick-with-it" rules of thumb:

✦ Some people are accustomed to pulling steaks right out of the refrigerator and putting them into the skillet still cold. Others, and I am one, prefer to let the steaks sit out until they reach room temperature. Either way is good, just do it the same way every time. Naturally, steaks at room temperature will cook quicker. Consistent timing and taste are going to be difficult to achieve if you do them cold one time and at room temperature the next. Find your way, and stick with it.

✦ Find a thickness of steaks you like, and stick with it. You'll be more consistent in your cooking times. A steak 1 to 1 1/2 inches thick is a good size for cooking.

✦ Use the same pan or skillet each time. Different pans and skillets vary in thickness and temperatures. Find a good one and stick with it. The same goes for your oven.

✦ Also, I always dust my steak in flour, which seals up the pores and holds in the juices; I always use the same kind of oil; and, I always complete the cooking process with Black Magic Finishing Sauce (page 41). As a simple guide, for 8 ounces of steak approximately 1 1/2 inches thick:

(a) Rub 1/2 teaspoon Texas Sprinkle (page 42) evenly over the meat.

(b) Dust the steak in 4 teaspoons flour.

(c) In a skillet, heat 2 tablespoons oil of your choice to hot, and brown the steak on both sides, cooking it to your preference.

(d) Add 1 teaspoon Black Magic Finishing Sauce on one side, flip the steak, and add 1 teaspoon to the other side—about 45 seconds to 1 minute before removing the steak from the fire. Total cooking time for a medium-rare steak 1 1/2 inches thick is 3 1/2 to 4 minutes.

✛ The same preparations apply for cooking venison on a stove, except that deer meat should be about $1/2$ inch thick and should be cooked no more than $1\,1/2$ minutes on each side. Venison is at its best medium rare.

Cowboy-Style Round Steak

Any ol' cowboy knows that the Colt Single Action pistol is the perfect weight (2 pounds) for pounding steak, and the shape of the butt is also ideal for pounding.

But you can't have more than 5 shells in the cylinder. And make sure the hammer is falling over the empty chamber so you don't shoot yourself in the gut.

Hold the pistol 4 to 6 inches over the steak and simply drop the handle onto the meat, in a hammering motion, to pound it out.

Of course, if you don't have a Colt, a Coca-Cola bottle will do just fine.

Makes 4 to 6 servings (about 2 servings per pound of steak)

Approximately 1 teaspoon peppercorn per pound of steak	Vegetable shortening, vegetable oil, or lard, for frying
Approximately 1/4 cup flour per pound of steak	
4 (8-, 10- or 12-ounce) round steaks (depending on how loudly your belly is growling)	

Crush the peppercorns on a cutting board with a rolling pin. Sprinkle the flour on the board over the pepper. Roll the steaks on the board several times to dust them with flour and pick up the pepper.

Pound out the steaks with a pistol, bottle, or the instrument of your choice, to three quarters of their original thickness. Heat the grease in a skillet, preferably cast iron, to a depth of 1/4 inch, until it is smoking hot (375°). Brown the steaks, one at a time, on both sides and keep them warm until all are cooked. Adjust the salt to taste, and serve.

Serving Suggestion:

+ Do not forget the "treasures" in the skillet—the drippings for pan gravy, if desired.

Matt Martinez's Culinary Frontier

Chalupas

Chalupas were the original taco salads. Cooks eventually started experimenting, using flour shells, puffed shells, too many ingredients. I prefer this simple method over any of the fancy taco salads of today.

Makes 4 servings

8	flat-fried corn tortillas (page 87)		1	cup coarsely chopped tomatoes
2	cups Refried or Cowboy Open-Range Beans No. 1 (pages 99 and 96)		2	cups shredded brisket or chicken, optional
2	cups shredded Monterey Jack or American cheese			Sweet white onion and jalapeños, sliced, as a garnish
3	cups chopped lettuce			

After frying the shells, spread equal amounts of the cooked beans and cheese evenly on top.

Heat the oven to 375°. Place the chalupas in a large baking dish and bake for 4 to 5 minutes, until the cheese melts.

Remove the dish from the oven and sprinkle some lettuce, tomatoes and meat over each chalupa. Serve immediately, garnished with the sliced jalapeños and onions.

Optional:

◆ Cover the top of the baked chalupas with the hot sauce of your choice and some Traditional Guacamole (page 62).

Matt's Favorite Fried Chicken

This is not the standard method of frying chicken—it's my recipe. Marinating the chicken in buttermilk and onion moistens and tenderizes it.

If you follow the "grease suggestion" at the bottom of the recipe, I don't see how you can eat any better fried chicken than this, but I've added a couple more fried chicken recipes, just in case.

Following those are 2 recipes for making gravy for fried chicken. One is the traditional way; the other is for "special occasion" gravy.

By the way, the following technique can also be used to fry $^3/_4$- to 1-inch-thick pork chops or loins.

Makes 4 to 6 servings

1–2	fryers (2$^1/_2$–3 pounds)	2	teaspoons salt
3	cups buttermilk	1$^1/_2$	teaspoons black pepper
1	medium sweet white onion, coarsely chopped	2	pounds vegetable shortening (Crisco, if available)
3	cups flour		

Wash the chicken, and cut it into serving pieces. Marinate the pieces in the refrigerator in air-tight plastic storage bags with the onion and buttermilk for 4 to 6 hours. Discard the excess buttermilk by pouring it through a strainer. Discard the onion pieces.

Mix together the flour, salt, and pepper. Roll the chicken in the seasoned flour.

Heat the shortening in a large, high-sided skillet, preferably cast iron, to no more than 350°. Do not allow the grease to get above half-deep in the skillet. Fry the chicken in the hot oil without crowding the skillet. The chicken is usually done when it starts floating and is golden brown. This takes 12 to 15 minutes per piece. Each time a piece is ready, transfer it to a 150° oven while cooking the remaining pieces, or while making gravy (page 180).

Grease Suggestions:

✤ To really drive your taste buds crazy in a happy way, mix the Crisco with 1 cup of bacon drippings. Once you've brought the grease up to frying temperature, add 1 onion, coarsely chopped; 1 green bell pepper, coarsely chopped; 3 cloves garlic, crushed; and 4 strips of bacon.

✤ As the vegetables start to brown, discard them. Remove the bacon when it's crisp. Now, you've flavored your grease and you're ready to do some serious frying.

✤ This "drive 'em crazy" grease is also great for frying fish.

Extra-Crispy Fried Chicken

Here's a chicken that I swear will almost make the skin pop in your mouth.

Makes 4 to 6 servings

1–2	fryers (2½–3 pounds each)		1½	teaspoons salt
2	cups water		1	teaspoon black pepper
	Juice of 1 lemon		2	pounds vegetable shortening (Crisco, if available)
2	cups flour			

Wash the chicken and cut it into serving pieces. In a bowl, combine the water, lemon juice, and chicken. Toss well. In a bowl, mix together the flour, salt, and pepper. Roll the chicken pieces in the flour mixture. Shake off the excess flour, and let the chicken sit on a cookie sheet or on paper towels for 5 to 10 minutes, then roll the chicken in the flour again.

Place the shortening in a large, high-sided skillet, preferably cast iron. Do not allow the grease to get above half-deep in the skillet.

Heat the oil to 350°, and fry the chicken in batches, without crowding the pan. The chicken is usually done when it starts floating and is golden brown. This takes 12 to 15 minutes per piece.

Each time a piece is ready, transfer it to a 150° oven to keep warm while cooking the remaining pieces, or while making chicken gravy (see page 180).

Grease Suggestion:

✚ For a devilishly wonderful taste, see the grease suggestion for Matt's Favorite Fried Chicken above.

Standard South Texas Fried Chicken

This is the traditional South Texas recipe. In the early days of Matt's El Rancho in Austin, Mom served this fried chicken. From the time the doors swung open in 1952, it was among the most popular plate-lunch specials.

Makes 4 to 6 servings

1–2 fryers (2½–3 pounds)	3 cups flour
6 eggs	2 pounds vegetable shortening (Crisco, if available)
1 cup whole milk	
Salt and black pepper, to taste	

Wash the chicken and cut it into serving pieces. In a bowl, whisk together the eggs and milk. Generously salt and pepper the chicken, then roll it in the flour.

Dip the chicken in the egg and milk mixture. Roll the chicken in the flour once more for good measure.

Place the shortening in a large, high-sided skillet, preferably cast iron. Do not allow the grease to get above half-deep in the skillet.

Heat the shortening to 350°, and fry the chicken in batches, without crowding the pan. The chicken is usually done when it starts floating and is golden brown. This takes 12 to 15 minutes per piece.

Each time a piece is ready, transfer it to a 150° oven to keep warm while cooking the remaining pieces, or while making chicken gravy (see below).

Grease Suggestion:

✚ If in search of paradise, use the grease suggestion for Matt's Favorite Fried Chicken (page 176)

Traditional Chicken Gravy

Pour this traditional gravy over your fried chicken; or, put it in a bowl on the side and dunk your pieces into the gravy. It's nothing fancy, but it sure is good.

Enough gravy for 2 fryers

- 2 tablespoons reserved chicken grease from pan
- 2 tablespoons flour
- 1 cup evaporated milk

- 1 cup water
- Salt and black pepper, to taste

Drain all but 2 tablespoons of grease from the pan after frying the chicken. On medium heat, add the flour. With a spatula, mix and loosen the bits and pieces as you brown the flour.

Add the milk and water to the flour and grease. Simmer on low heat, stirring, for 1 to 2 minutes.

Season with the salt and pepper.

Special Occasion Chicken Gravy

Here's a gravy worth making for the holidays or other special occasions. It's a little heavier than the preceding gravy. The mushrooms and onions give it more flavor, too.

Enough gravy for 2 fryers

- 3 tablespoons reserved chicken grease from pan
- 3 tablespoons flour
- 1 cup finely chopped sweet white onions

- 1 cup finely chopped mushrooms (portobello, if available)
- 3 cups whole milk
- Salt and black pepper, to taste

Drain all but 3 tablespoons of grease from the pan after frying the chicken. On medium heat, add the flour, onions, and mushrooms.

With a spoon or spatula, mix and loosen the bits and pieces as you brown the flour and vegetables for 2 to 3 minutes. Add the milk and continue to stir on low heat. Let the gravy simmer, stirring, for another 1 to 2 minutes.

Season with the salt and pepper.

Serving Suggestion:

✦ For tears of joy, spoon this gravy over white rice.

REMEMBERING EL RANCHO AND YESTERDAY

Darrell Royal

Darrell was one of the most famous coaches in the history of college football. In his twenty seasons (1957–76) as head coach of the University of Texas, Darrell led the Longhorns to three national titles and eleven Southwest Conference championships, including six in a row. He frequented El Rancho every step of the way, and still does.

First time I ate at El Rancho, it was the little frame house at East First and San Jacinto. That was forty years ago. I'd heard of Mexican food, but I'd never heard of Tex-Mex. I'd travel and go no farther than El Paso or New Mexico, and the Mexican food would change drastically; it just wasn't the same.

Another thing about El Rancho, Matt [Senior] always made you feel welcome. He always shook your hand and had that big smile. He didn't stand and chat or get in your way, but he certainly greeted you, gave you the big smile, and said "Thank you" on the way out.

VII

Seafood,
Wild Game,
Prairie
Specialties

Roasted Armadillo (Poor-Man's Pig)

Harvesting time for armadillos is late November through February. Don't shoot the big breeders; they taste too gamey. The young, tender ones have the sweet meat that tastes like pork.

Makes 4 servings

2¹/₂–3 pounds yearling armadillo	1 teaspoon cayenne pepper
¹/₂ cup olive oil	1 tablespoon cornstarch
1 tablespoon Texas Sprinkle (page 42)	
1 tablespoon chili powder	

Preheat the oven to 325°. Rub the armadillo with the oil. Mix the sprinkle with the dry ingredients, and evenly coat the armadillo.

Place the armadillo on the rack of a roasting pan, cover it tightly with aluminum foil, and roast for approximately 3 hours. Uncover during the last 30 minutes of cooking to brown lightly. Serve with steamed rice or buttered noodles.

Chicken-Fried Breast of Dove (or Goose or Chicken)

As far as I know, I have eaten every species of bird to fly over Texas. Which, now that the statute of limitations has expired, leads me to a confession.

I have eaten 3 mockingbirds.

Because the mockingbird is the state bird of Texas, it is, of course, illegal to kill one, let alone eat 3.

For those of you wondering, roadrunners and mockingbirds taste exactly the same. So, do yourself a favor, stay within the law and cook up a roadrunner instead.

Somewhere along about 1955, I was a boy out hunting with a friend, and my friend shot a sparrow. That made me jealous. I set up under a chinaberry tree and waited to bag one of my own.

Low and behold, in flies a mockingbird. I popped him good and plucked him real quick.

We wrapped our little birds in foil and laid them in some coals over dirt. Two hours later, we were ready to dine.

His bird came out perfect. Mine? Tough as a boot.

In the ensuing months, I bagged a couple more and ate them, too, of course. Looking back on it all, I do regret having eaten those mockingbirds.

But if I had it all to do over again, I think I would have cooked them just a little longer.

In the meantime, here's a recipe for chicken-fried dove. It works just as well on goose and chicken. No more mockingbirds, please. I'm beginning to feel a little guilty just thinking about them.

Makes 4 servings

1 1/2–2 pounds boned dove breast
        (or goose or chicken)

2 cups buttermilk

    Oil of your choice (peanut or
    canola is best), for frying

1 cup flour (or, 1/2 cup flour, 1/2 cup
   cornmeal for a crispier crust)

1 teaspoon salt

1/2 teaspoon black pepper

1 recipe Perfect Cream Gravy
   (page 43)

Marinate the breasts in the buttermilk for 6 to 24 hours.

Pour in enough oil to come halfway up the sides of a big pot or skillet. While heating the oil to 375°, combine the flour, salt, and pepper on a plate. Coat the breasts in the flour mixture.

Deep-fry the breasts in the oil for 3 to 4 minutes. They are ready when they float. Do not overcook the meat, or it will be tough. Drain the breasts on paper towels. Serve with the cream gravy on the side.

Quail

The first quail I ever shot was with my Daisy Scout BB gun—back when it was my most treasured rifle. I was feeling sorta proud, so I took the bird to my granny, Maria Gaytan. She prepared it for cooking, dusted it in flour, cooked it in a black skillet, and cut it 4 ways.

Might have been the best bird I've ever eaten. And you know what I liked most about it? The trophy was on the plate, not on the wall. Any quail shot by a Martinez went right into Granny's skillet.

Makes 4 servings

3 slices of bacon	1/2 teaspoon black pepper, plus extra, to taste
8 quail, or 2 pounds other wild bird	2 teaspoons crushed and finely chopped garlic
3 tablespoons flour	
1/2 cup finely chopped onion	3 teaspoons ground cumin
1/2 cup finely chopped green bell pepper	1 tablespoon soy sauce
	1 tablespoon brandy or whiskey
1/4 cup finely chopped celery	4 cups water
2 cups finely chopped fresh mushrooms	1 cup crushed tomatoes
2 cups fresh or frozen corn kernels	Chopped green onion, as a garnish
1 teaspoon salt, plus extra, to taste	

In a skillet, sauté the bacon until crisp. Chop into small pieces. Leave 3 tablespoons of bacon drippings in the pan, and reserve the crumbled bacon bits.

Dust the quail in the flour, then sauté them in the bacon drippings for 4 to 5 minutes, or until the quail have browned.

Combine the onion, bell pepper, celery, mushrooms, corn, teaspoon of salt, 1/2 teaspoon black pepper, garlic, and cumin in the pan. Remove the quail.

Lightly sauté the vegetables for 2 to 3 minutes, until they are translucent. Add the soy sauce and brandy or whiskey, and sauté for 30 seconds to 1 minute. When it's all sautéed, add the water and crushed tomatoes.

Bring the sauce to a simmer, add the quail, and cover the pan (add more water, too, if dry; the sauce should be thick and pourable, but not lumpy). Simmer the quail for 30 minutes, or until they are tender.

Adjust the salt and pepper. Sprinkle the bacon bits on top, and garnish with chopped green onion.

Serving Suggestion:

+ For maximum mouth-watering effect, serve quail over steamed rice or buttered pasta.

Breast of Quail Fajitas

Here's a fine example of how to incorporate an old prairie-style favorite—quail in a skillet—with something only about 20 years old—the making of fajitas.

Dove, turkey, or chicken may be substituted for the quail.

Makes 2 to 4 servings

- 1 batch Vegetable Fajitas (page 119)
- 1 pound meat (10–12 quail), cut into ¹/₂-inch strips
- 1 cup combination of sweet white onion and red or green bell pepper cut into ¹/₂-inch strips
- 1¹/₄ teaspoons Texas Sprinkle (page 42)

- 2 tablespoons vegetable oil, or 1 tablespoon bacon drippings and 1 tablespoon vegetable oil (best)
- 1 tablespoon Black Magic Finishing Sauce (page 41)
- 6–8 flour or corn tortillas

Prepare the Vegetable Fajitas and keep them warm in the oven while cooking the rest.

In a bowl, combine the meat, onion–bell pepper combination, and Texas Sprinkle. In a skillet, heat the oil to smoking hot. Splash 1 or 2 droplets of water in a corner of the skillet; if it "spits" back, the oil is ready.

Sauté the meat and onion–pepper combination in the hot skillet for about 2 minutes, until evenly browned. Make sure the meat is done all the way through by breaking open one piece with a spatula or fork. Add the Black Magic and sauté for 30 seconds.

Load and wrap a soft tortilla with meat, onion and bell pepper strips, Vegetable Fajitas, and the usual fajita accompaniments: hot sauce of your choice, Chile con Queso (page 59), Traditional Guacamole (page 62), tomatoes, and Pico de Gallo (page 46). One batch of each accompaniment should easily do for 4 servings.

Serving Suggestion:
+ Refried Beans (page 99) go great with all fajitas.

Shrimp Fajitas

Jumbo shrimp are best for fajitas. Smaller shrimp may not stand up to the other multitude of tastes you've got wrapped up. You can always chop up the big shrimp before filling your tortillas.

Makes 4 plump fajitas

1 batch Vegetable Fajitas (page 119)	2 tablespoons vegetable oil, or 1 tablespoon bacon drippings and 1 tablespoon vegetable oil (best)
1¼ pounds raw jumbo shrimp (20 count—Gulf Coast is best)	
1 cup combination of sweet white onion and red or green bell pepper cut into ½-inch strips	1 tablespoon Black Magic Finishing Sauce (page 41)
	6–8 flour or corn tortillas
1¼ teaspoons Texas Sprinkle (page 42)	

Prepare the Vegetable Fajitas and keep them warm in the oven while cooking the rest.

Shell, clean, and devein the shrimp. In a bowl, combine the shrimp, onion–bell pepper combination, and Texas Sprinkle.

In a skillet, heat the oil to smoking hot. Splash 1 or 2 droplets of water in a corner of the skillet; if it "spits" back, the oil is ready.

Sauté the shrimp mixture in the hot skillet for 2½ to 3 minutes, until the shrimp change color. Be careful not to overcook the shrimp. Add the Black Magic and sauté for 30 seconds.

Load and wrap a soft tortilla with the shrimp mixture (chop the shrimp up if and how you prefer), Vegetable Fajitas, and the usual fajita accompaniments: hot sauce of your choice, Chile con Queso (page 59), Traditional Guacamole (page 62), tomatoes, and Pico de Gallo (page 46). One batch of each (or any of the above) should easily do for 4 servings.

Serving Suggestion:
+ Refried Beans (page 99) go great with all fajitas.

Venison Fajitas

Ask any avid hunter in the country what deer he or she most covets, and the treasure of them all is the Trophy whitetail.

I feel fortunate that Jim Jensen, the hunter who brought in the biggest whitetail of them all, invited me to go hunting with him in Saskatchewan, Canada, in the winter of 1995.

Mr. Jensen seems to feel the same way about hunting that I do. Most hunters get caught up in fueling their machismo. They gauge their hunting prowess by the number of antlers, horns, and hooves they take from bucks. Because the bucks are the ones with the antlers, that's what most hunters pursue.

And that's why we've gotten away from the real reasons we hunt.

Nowadays, sportsmen hunt for trophy rather than out of respect for the meat. I want us to put the trophy on the plate—at least until the eating begins.

Deer are best harvested, all fat and sassy, early in the season. Properly harvested and processed venison avoid that wild-game taste that has been known to run some off. You may substitute red meat or emu for Venison Fajitas.

Makes 2 to 4 servings

1 batch Vegetable Fajitas (page 119)	1 cup combination of sweet white onion and red or green bell pepper cut into 1/2-inch strips
1 1/4 teaspoons Texas Sprinkle (page 42)	1 tablespoon Black Magic Finishing Sauce (page 41)
1 pound venison, cut into 1/2-inch-thick strips	6–8 flour or corn tortillas
2 tablespoons vegetable oil, or 1 tablespoon bacon drippings and 1 tablespoon vegetable oil (best)	

Prepare the Vegetable Fajitas and keep them warm in the oven while cooking the rest.

Sprinkle the Texas Sprinkle evenly over the venison. In a skillet, heat the oil to smoking hot. Splash 1 or 2 droplets of water in a corner of the skillet; if it "spits" back, the oil is ready.

Matt Martinez's Culinary Frontier

Sauté the onion–bell pepper combination in the hot oil for 45 seconds to 1 minute. Still on very high heat, add the venison and continue tossing for 2 minutes. The meat should be evenly brown on all sides, but be careful not to overcook it.

Add the Black Magic and continue tossing for 30 seconds. The venison should be perfect when medium rare. The entire cooking process should take $3^1/_2$ to 4 minutes. Load and wrap a soft tortilla with meat, onion and bell pepper strips, Vegetable Fajitas, and the usual fajita accompaniments: hot sauce of your choice, Chile con Queso (page 59), Traditional Guacamole (page 62), tomatoes, and Pico de Gallo (page 46). One batch of each (or any of the above) should easily do for 4 servings.

Serving Suggestion:
+ Refried Beans (page 99) go great with all fajitas.

Shrimp Enchiladas with Ranchero Salsa

Tomatillo Salsa and sour cream go so well together; but, I like the way the Ranchero Salsa and sour cream team up with shrimp for a full range of tastes in this enchilada.

Makes 2 to 4 servings (8 enchiladas)

1 batch Ranchero Salsa (page 31)	8 tablespoons sour cream
1 cup vegetable oil	2 cups grated Monterey Jack or Swiss cheese
8 corn tortillas	1 tablespoon freshly grated Parmesan cheese
1 1/4 pounds raw jumbo shrimp (20 count—Gulf Coast is best)	
3 tablespoons butter	

After you've made the salsa, heat the oil in a skillet on medium heat. With tongs, carefully swipe each tortilla through the grease, no more than 2 seconds. Drag the tortilla over the side of the skillet, removing the excess grease, and stack the tortillas on a warm plate. One by one, dip the tortillas into the salsa and stack them again on the plate.

Shell, clean, and devein the shrimp, then cube them into 1/4-inch chunks. Preheat the oven to 350°.

In a skillet, melt the butter on high heat. Once the butter bubbles, add the shrimp and cook on high for 45 seconds to 1 minute. Stir the shrimp in the butter and remove the skillet from the heat; the shrimp will continue to cook off the fire. Spread 1 tablespoon of sour cream evenly inside each tortilla. Divide the shrimp among the 8 tortillas, spreading them along the center, and then tightly roll up each tortilla.

Arrange the enchiladas in a 12-inch oven-proof dish. Spread the remaining salsa over them and sprinkle on some Monterey Jack or Swiss cheese. Mix the Swiss and Monterey Jack, if you like. Bake the enchiladas for 15 to 20 minutes, until the cheese is completely melted. Sprinkle the Parmesan on top just before serving.

Shrimp Martinez

This recipe has been an Austin favorite at Matt's El Rancho since Mom and Dad put it on the menu in 1962. Beware: Shrimp are too often overcooked.

Makes 4 servings

- 8 teaspoons vegetable oil or other oil of your choice
- 2 teaspoons Texas Sprinkle (page 42)
- 1 pound raw peeled and cleaned jumbo shrimp (20 count—I prefer Gulf Coast)

- 4 heaping tablespoons flour
- 4 teaspoons Black Magic Finishing Sauce (page 41)

In a large skillet, preferably cast iron, heat the oil to 375°. Apply the Texas Sprinkle to the shrimp, then dust them in the flour.

Carefully place the dusted shrimp in the hot oil, and cook them on high heat until they evenly and completely change color (some shrimp turn white, others pink). This will take 3 to 4 minutes, depending on the size of the shrimp. When the shrimp are cooked to perfection, splash them with Black Magic and serve them immediately.

Optional:

◆ For more character, before splashing on the Black Magic, add to the skillet 4 tablespoons *each* sliced portobello mushrooms, onion, and peppers (mild or hot); and 4 teaspoons crumbled fried bacon. Toss, add the Black Magic, and serve.

Serving Suggestions:

✦ As an entrée, Shrimp Martinez is enhanced by steamed rice, pastas, vegetables, or skillet spinach.

✦ This recipe may also be used as an appetizer, depending on the quantity you are making.

Frog Legs Martinez

These days, I prefer to buy my frog legs. When you're out hunting for frogs, you and some snake are usually after the same thing—a fat frog—and an unhappy snake makes my poor heart go pitter-patter a little more than I can stand. Besides, we usually run out of beer and whiskey, which means our eyes can get a little blurry and our frog gigs have a way of losing their accuracy.

Frog Legs Martinez is a great entrée or appetizer. You decide by the quantity. Frog legs do differ in size. The best way is to use this formula for every 4 ounces of frog.

Makes 1 serving per 8 ounces frog legs (6–8 pair per pound)

Per 4 Ounces of Legs:

- 2 teaspoons vegetable oil or other oil of your choice
- 1/2 teaspoon Texas Sprinkle (page 42)
- 1 heaping tablespoon flour
- 1 teaspoon Black Magic Finishing Sauce (page 41)

In a large skillet, preferably cast iron, heat the oil to 350°. Apply the Texas Sprinkle to the frog legs, then dust them with the flour.

Carefully place the dusted frog legs in the hot oil. Cook them for 3 to 5 minutes per side, until they are golden brown. To test if they are done, press the legs where they are joined with the side of a spoon; if they disjoint easily, they're ready.

Splash the frog legs with Black Magic, and serve them immediately.

Optional:

◆ For more character, before splashing on the Black Magic, add to the skillet 1 tablespoon *each* sliced portobello mushrooms, chopped onion, chopped peppers (mild or hot); and crumbled fried bacon. Toss, add the Black Magic, and serve.

Serving Suggestions:

✚ Serve Frog Legs Martinez over rice, pasta, vegetables, or grilled spinach.

Catfish Martinez

In the northern regions of our country, many people think of catfish as a garbage or trash fish because catfish found in their rivers and streams are known to eat anything they can suck up.

Farm-raised catfish are much different. They're probably the fish of the future. They're high in nutrition, low in fat, and kitchen-friendly: They're easy to work with.

I prefer the fillets over whole catfish. You can cook them many more ways. The fish of your choice—particularly bass, bream, crappie, perch, or trout—may be substituted for catfish in any of the following recipes.

Makes 4 servings

- 3 tablespoons vegetable oil or other oil of your choice
- 2 teaspoons Texas Sprinkle (page 42)
- 1–1 1/2 pounds farm-raised catfish fillets, fresh or frozen
- 4 heaping tablespoons flour
- 4 teaspoons Black Magic Finishing Sauce (page 41)

In a large skillet, preferably cast iron, heat the oil to 375°. Apply the Texas Sprinkle to the fillets, then dust them in the flour.

Place the dusted catfish in the hot oil, and cook them for 3 to 5 minutes on each side. They are ready when they are golden brown and soft enough to flake easily with a fork.

When the fillets are cooked to perfection, splash them with Black Magic, and serve them immediately.

Serving Suggestions:

✦ Serve Catfish Martinez over prepared rice, pasta, vegetables, or grilled spinach.

Matt Jr. and his sons, Matt III and Marco, show off their catfish catch.

Fried Catfish (also for Bass, Bream, Crappie, Perch, and Trout)

With all apologies to fat- and calorie-counters, this extra-crispy, cornmeal-breaded batter is best fried in a black skillet with lard.

Makes 8 to 10 servings (8 ounces of fish per person)

1/2 cup flour	1 teaspoon black pepper
1/2 cup cornstarch	4–5 pounds fish fillets
2 cups yellow cornmeal	Corn oil or lard, for deep frying
1 1/2 teaspoons salt	

For breading, mix the dry ingredients together on a plate.

Dip the fish fillets into cold water, soaking them on all sides, then roll the fillets in the breading.

Ease the fish into a fryer, or into hot grease at 375°. Depending on the size of your deep-fryer or skillet, use just under a half-skillet of fat. Fry the fillets for 3 to 4 minutes, until golden brown. The fish are ready when they float.

Honey Mustard Catfish

The sweet flavor of honey mustard really enhances this fish.

Makes 6 servings

1	teaspoon vegetable oil
1	cup chopped pecans
1 1/2–2	pounds (approximately 6 fillets) farm-raised catfish fillets, fresh or frozen and thawed
1	(4-ounce) jar (approximately 1/2 cup) honey mustard

3 tablespoons finely chopped green onion, as a garnish

1 lemon, sliced, as a garnish

Preheat the oven to 450° and grease a baking sheet.

Heat the vegetable oil in a skillet and roast the chopped pecans by sautéing them over medium heat 2 to 3 minutes until they are brown. Drain them on paper towels.

Place the fillets in a single layer on the baking sheet. Generously brush each fillet with some of the honey mustard.

Bake the fillets for 10 to 12 minutes, or until they flake easily with a fork.

Just before serving, sprinkle each fillet with some of the pecans. Use the onion and lemon slices as garnishes.

Catfish Creole

Technically speaking, a Creole is a white descendant of the French and Spanish who settled near the Gulf of Mexico, mainly in Louisiana and Texas's Golden Triangle area—Beaumont, Port Arthur, and Orange in Southeast Texas.

These people have preserved the dialect and culture of their forefathers, and they also know their way around a spice rack. Their food is powerfully seasoned.

Cajun and Creole cooking are actually two different cuisines. Cajun cooking is from the country; Creole is more sophisticated and was developed in New Orleans by the city's aristocratic settlers.

Makes 6 servings

1 1/2–2 pounds (approximately 6 fillets) farm-raised catfish fillets, fresh or frozen and thawed	1/4 bay leaf
1/4 cup butter	1 tablespoon fresh lemon juice
1/4 cup finely chopped green onion	1 (16-ounce) can stewed crushed tomatoes
2 tablespoons finely chopped fresh flat-leaf parsley	1/2 teaspoon salt
2 cloves garlic, crushed and minced	1/2 teaspoon cayenne pepper

Pat the catfish fillets dry with paper towels and place them in a baking dish.

In a saucepan, melt the butter. Add the green onion, parsley, and garlic, and sauté for only 30 seconds to 1 minute.

Add the bay leaf, lemon juice, tomatoes, salt, and cayenne, and simmer the sauce for 45 minutes, stirring occasionally. Discard the bay leaf.

Preheat the oven to 325°. Pour the sauce over the fillets in the baking dish, and bake them for about 20 minutes, or until the fish flakes easily with a fork.

Catfish Spaghetti

Sometimes I wonder what the people of Italy ate before Marco Polo went out and made a name for himself. They got pasta from the Orientals and many of their vegetables, peppers, and tomatoes from the New World. Before then, those folks must have been starving to death.

What really gets my goat is when I see a label for an Italian plum tomato or some other kind of Italian tomato. Hey, they got them from America. That's the Roma tomato, the wild tomato that grew all over the place in certain regions of Texas. Now, they call them Italian tomatoes. Give me a break.

Here's a spaghetti recipe, straight from the heart of Texas, more or less.

Makes 4 to 6 servings

1/4 cup butter or margarine	1 teaspoon salt
1 1/2–2 pounds (approximately 6 fillets) farm-raised catfish fillets, fresh or frozen and thawed	1/2 teaspoon black pepper (fresh ground is best)
1 tablespoon finely chopped garlic	12–16 ounces spaghetti, cooked and drained
8 ounces fresh mushrooms, sliced	1 cup freshly grated Parmesan cheese
1/2 cup chopped fresh flat-leaf parsley	Lemon slices (optional)
1/2 cup white wine	Fresh parsley sprigs (optional)
2 tablespoons fresh lemon juice	

Melt the butter or margarine in your favorite skillet. Cut the fillets into bite-size pieces, and add them to the skillet along with the garlic. Sauté for 5 minutes, stirring occasionally.

Add the mushrooms and parsley, and sauté for 3 minutes, stirring occasionally. Add the wine, lemon juice, salt, and pepper. Simmer for 12 minutes and continue to stir occasionally.

When the fillets flake easily with a fork, spoon them over the cooked spaghetti. Sprinkle on the Parmesan cheese, and, if desired, garnish with the lemon slices and parsley sprigs.

All-American Catfish Vegetable Skillet

Remember, you may substitute fillets of bass, bream, crappie, perch, or trout—if you have not yet learned to love catfish—for any of these fish recipes. The day will surely come when catfish is your choice.

These recipes are flexible, and suitable for the fish of your region.

Makes 4 to 6 servings

1 1/2 tablespoons plus 1 teaspoon vegetable oil

1/2 cup chopped pecans

1 cup sliced mushrooms (I prefer portobellos)

3 cups frozen cut green beans (1/2 cup per serving)

1/2 cup coarsely chopped red bell pepper, plus 18 thinly sliced strips

1/4 teaspoon salt, plus extra, to taste

1/2 teaspoon black pepper, plus extra, to taste

1 1/2–2 pounds (approximately 6 fillets) farm-raised catfish fillets, fresh or frozen and thawed

Freshly grated Parmesan cheese, to taste

3 slices of bacon, fried and crumbled, as a garnish

In a skillet, heat the teaspoon of oil and roast the chopped pecans by sautéing them over medium heat until they are brown, about 2 to 3 minutes. Drain them on paper towels.

In a large, nonstick skillet, heat the remaining oil over medium heat to 350°. Add the mushrooms, green beans, chopped (not the sliced) red bell pepper, 1/4 teaspoon salt, and 1/2 teaspoon pepper, and sauté them for 1 to 2 minutes.

Place the fish fillets over the vegetable mixture. Add more salt and pepper. Garnish each fillet with 3 strips of red bell pepper.

Cover the skillet and cook the fillets over medium heat for approximately 12 minutes, or until the fish flakes easily with a fork.

Remove the skillet from the heat and lightly sprinkle each fillet with some cheese. Sprinkle the roasted pecans over the vegetables and fish. Off the fire, cover the skillet again, and let the fish stand a minute or two, until the cheese melts. Garnish with the bacon crumbs. Serve the fillets and vegetables immediately, right from the skillet. Or, arrange them attractively on a warm platter.

REMEMBERING EL RANCHO AND YESTERDAY

David Gaytan

David is Matt Jr.'s uncle. He is the son of Maria Gaytan and brother to Matt's mother, Janie. Often, David took Little Matt fishing or playing while Matt's parents operated El Rancho.

My fathered died in an accident in 1932, and my mother was left alone to care for five children during the Depression. We had two cows, some chickens, and one acre of land, including a garden.

My mother was a real go-getter. She began making homemade-brewed beer, back when it was illegal to sell liquor. On Saturdays,

Uncle Dave and Aunt Delores Gaytan, from Brownsville. Uncle Dave always took Matt Jr. fishing.

when we children had no chores, we would go to market in Round Rock, five miles from our old home, and buy the yeast and malt and whatever she needed to make the beer.

She made moonshine in a twenty-gallon drum and sold it at five cents a bottle to farmers and others who would come up from Austin to buy it. That money helped us scrape by.

Competing bootleggers in the area got greedy and threatened to tell the law. One time, me, my brother, and some neighbors picked up the twenty-gallon drum and put it on a cart and hid it in the woods beneath some cedar limbs. When we went back to get it, the still was bubbling away.

We would cool the beer off in a tub of ice. And after it fermented, we would put the bottles of beer on the shady side of the house.

My mother was her own maker, bottler, and distributor of beer, all for five cents a bottle.

Deviled-Baked Catfish

If you don't get all starry-eyed and if angels do not appear at the moment you take your first bite of this catfish, then perhaps the devil made you do it.

As a rule of thumb, I use soft bread crumbs, not dry ones. Soft crumbs create a different texture. They are made by lightly tearing the bread into tiny pieces with your fingers or a fork. A blender or food processor will also do.

Makes 6 servings

2 tablespoons butter or margarine	1 1/2–2 pounds (approximately 6 fillets) farm-raised catfish fillets, fresh or frozen and thawed
1/4 cup coarsely chopped red bell pepper	Salt and black pepper, to taste
1 clove garlic, crushed and chopped	1/2 cup shredded Monterey Jack cheese
1 cup soft bread crumbs (see headnote), loosely packed	
1/4 cup mayonnaise	
2 tablespoons prepared mustard (I prefer French's)	

Preheat the oven to 350°. Butter a 3-quart shallow baking dish.

In a 10-inch skillet, melt the butter and sauté the bell peppers and garlic for approximately 5 minutes, stirring occasionally. Lightly stir in the bread crumbs, mayonnaise, and mustard until everything is blended. Remove the skillet from the heat.

Arrange the fish fillets in the baking dish and season them with salt and pepper. Spoon the bread crumb mixture over the fish, and sprinkle with the cheese. Bake the fillets for 20 to 30 minutes, or until they flake easily with a fork. Do *not* overbake. Serve immediately.

Catfish Kabobs

Foil must be placed on the pit's grate for these kabobs, or you may spend some of your cooking time digging pieces of flaked-off catfish out of the coals.

Makes 4 to 6 servings

1 1/2–2 pounds fresh or frozen and thawed farm-raised catfish fillets, cut into 1-x-3-inch strips

8 ounces whole fresh mushrooms

2 large green bell peppers, cut into 1-inch chunks

18 cherry tomatoes

18 pearl onions, or 2 large white onions, cut into chunks

1 (16-ounce) can pineapple chunks packed in their own juice

1/4 cup vegetable oil

1 tablespoon curry powder

1 tablespoon soy sauce

1/4 teaspoon black pepper

1 teaspoon salt

1/2 cup cranberry juice

On 12 or more skewers, arrange the catfish, folded into chunks, along with the mushrooms, bell peppers, tomatoes, onions, and pineapple. Place the skewers in several large air-tight plastic storage bags.

In a large mixing bowl, combine the oil, curry powder, soy sauce, pepper, salt, and cranberry juice. Pour the marinade into the bags, seal the bags, and refrigerate 4 to 6 hours.

Place enough coals in a barbecue pit to cook 12 skewers of kabobs. While waiting for the coals to reach moderate heat, puncture numerous tiny holes in a sheet of aluminum foil. Place the foil on the grate.

Remove the kabobs from the marinade and place them on the foil over the coals. Cook the kabobs for 15 to 20 minutes, turning occasionally, until the fish flakes easily with a fork.

Serving Suggestions:
+ Serve the kabobs over rice or noodles.
+ Potato salad makes a great side dish.

Creek Bottom Catfish

Once you have prepared and built Creek Bottom Catfish on your plate, notice how the bed of rice, spinach, vegetables, and chopped shrimp take on the appearance of a somewhat murky creek bottom for the catfish. The tastes really blend together in a wonderful way.

Makes 4 to 6 servings

1	cup uncooked Uncle Ben's wild rice mix		8	teaspoons Black Magic Finishing Sauce (page 41)
1	(8-ounce) bag fresh spinach, stemmed and thoroughly washed		1	cup coarsely chopped portobello mushrooms
7	teaspoons Texas Sprinkle (page 42)		1	cup coarsely chopped sweet white onions
1 1/2–2	pounds fresh or frozen and thawed catfish fillets		1	cup mixed coarsely chopped red and green bell peppers
12–16	raw jumbo shrimp (20 count), peeled and chopped (I prefer Gulf Coast)		1	cup coarsely chopped jalapeño (optional)
6	heaping tablespoons flour		4	slices of bacon, crispy fried and crumbled
1/2	cup vegetable oil or other oil of your choice (not olive)			

Prepare the rice according to the directions on the package. In a pot, blanche the spinach in boiling water for about 30 seconds, until it is wilted. Drain at once. Sprinkle 4 teaspoons of the Texas Sprinkle over the catfish and shrimp. Dust the catfish with the flour.

In a skillet, preferably cast iron, heat 8 teaspoons of oil and brown the catfish on both sides on medium-high heat for 3 to 4 minutes total. When both sides are browned, splash on 4 teaspoons of the Black Magic. Remove the fillets from the skillet and keep them warm in the oven.

In the same skillet, add the remaining 4 teaspoons of oil, as well as the remaining 3 teaspoons of Texas Sprinkle, and sauté the vegetables for 2 to 3 minutes, until the onions are translucent. Add the shrimp and bacon bits. Cook over high heat for 3 to 4 minutes, until the shrimp changes color. At the very end of cooking, add the remaining 4 teaspoons of Black Magic.

To complete, layer on a warmed serving plate thusly: First, make a bed of rice; then top the rice with the spinach; top the spinach with the catfish; and, top the catfish with the vegetables and chopped shrimp. Serve immediately.

Farm-Raised Catfish Jambalaya

My Cajun cooking buddies have a way of dishing out food that sweats out all fevers, hangovers, whatever's ailing you.

This jambalaya will also do the trick.

Makes 4 to 6 servings

6	slices of bacon, diced		1	(2-pound) can stewed tomatoes
1/2	pound sausage meat of your choice		1	tablespoon Worcestershire sauce
2	cups coarsely chopped onions		1	teaspoon salt, plus extra, to taste
2	cloves garlic, pressed and minced			Black pepper, to taste
1	cup coarsely chopped celery		1	tablespoon chili powder
1	cup coarsely chopped green bell peppers			
1 1/2–2	pounds (approximately 6 fillets) farm-raised catfish fillets, fresh or frozen and thawed			

In a large skillet, cook the bacon and sausage together until the bacon is crisp and the sausage is brown. Drain all but 4 tablespoons of the drippings.

Add the onions, garlic, celery, and green peppers to the bacon and sausage, and sauté for 1 minute. Add the catfish, and sauté for approximately 5 minutes on each side.

Add the stewed tomatoes, Worcestershire sauce, teaspoon salt, and the chili powder. Simmer for 10 minutes. Adjust the salt and the pepper. Serve immediately.

Serving Suggestions:

+ The jambalaya is great over rice, mashed potatoes, or noodles.

REMEMBERING EL RANCHO AND YESTERDAY

Matt Martínez, III

Matt is one of Matt and Estella's four grown children.

When I was six years old, I was waiting tables at El Rancho—serving tea and water, taking money to the cash register.

I got sick one day and couldn't go to school. My parents thought I'd had an allergic reaction to something, so they let me work at the restaurant that day.

We found out later I had chicken pox. Fortunately, I didn't spread it around. I don't think I did, anyway.

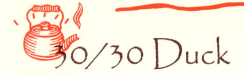

30/30 Duck

The name of this duck carries a double meaning. Not only do you roast it for 30 minutes at 500° and for another 30 at 400°, but the first duck I ever shot was with a 30/30 Winchester.

I was 14 years old and hunting deer with the Granbury boys, Tommy and H.B., near Buda, in the Texas Hill Country. It was a drizzly, ugly morning. The sun was just creeping over the horizon, trying hard to poke its rays through the haze.

I was sitting in an oak tree overlooking a big pond when I spotted this big-league duck.

By the time we'd be getting back to camp, the Granbury brothers and I knew we'd be hungry. We had already begun to think about food.

"Too cold for armadillos," H.B. had said.

"Ain't seen any rabbits," Tommy said, with a shrug.

So I shot the duck. Then I almost froze to death wading into the water. In fact, I had to go in deep enough that I figured I'd probably never be able to have children.

I thought the duck was an albino mallard, but it turned out to be a nearby neighbor's tame duck.

I took it back to camp and cooked it in 30-minute intervals. If it was still tough, I'd turn down the heat and cook it for another 30 minutes. I continued in that fashion until it was just right.

Eventually, I developed this 30/30 method by experimenting on a few store-bought ducks. The recipe is nothing fancy, just plain ol' duck-eatin' good.

Makes 2 to 4 servings

1	duckling (4¹/2–4³/4 pounds)	1	cup water
	Salt and black pepper, to taste		

Preheat the oven to 500°.

With a sharp knife, score the duck at 1-inch intervals. Trim all the loose fat around the opening in the neck. Generously salt and pepper the duck, and place it on a rack in a roasting pan. Pour the water into the duck cavity.

Roast the duck for 30 minutes at 500°. Turn the heat down to 400°, and continue cooking for another 30 minutes.

Without opening the oven, turn it off. Let the duck sit in the oven for 30 minutes more, then remove it and let it sit for an additional 10 to 15 minutes before carving.

Serving Suggestions:
+ Add the duck to salads, stews, or eat it as an entrée. Plain ol' duck is not too bad.

30/30 Duck with Brown Sauce

This brown sauce duck and the preceding plain ol' duck differ in taste and appearance. This one is skinned and boned and dressed up to look more fetching.

Makes 2 to 4 servings

1 cooked 30/30 Duck (see preceding recipe)	1/2 cup white wine (light, crisp Chenin Blanc works great)
4 tablespoons duck drippings	2 1/2 cups water or Chicken Broth (canned, or see page 47)
3 tablespoons flour	Salt and black pepper, to taste
1 cup coarsely chopped sweet white onions	
8 ounces portobellos or other mushrooms of your choice, sliced	

When the duck is cooked and has "rested," skin and bone it, then keep it warm in the oven.

Heat the duck drippings in the pan to medium heat. Add the flour and sauté for 3 to 4 minutes, stirring constantly.

Matt Jr., former Dallas Cowboys head coach Jimmy Johnson (now head coach of the Miami Dolphins), and Matt III discuss wild game and third-and-long situations.

Add the onions and mushrooms, and continue stirring until the vegetables start to brown lightly and cake. Add the wine and continue stirring for 1 minute, letting the wine steam while continuing to cook the onions and mushrooms.

Add the water or broth, then immediately add the duck meat.

Season with salt and pepper, and simmer on low heat for 5 to 10 minutes.

Adjust the thickness of the sauce by adding more broth, if necessary.

Serving Suggestion:

+ Serve the duck and brown sauce with steamed rice or noodles.

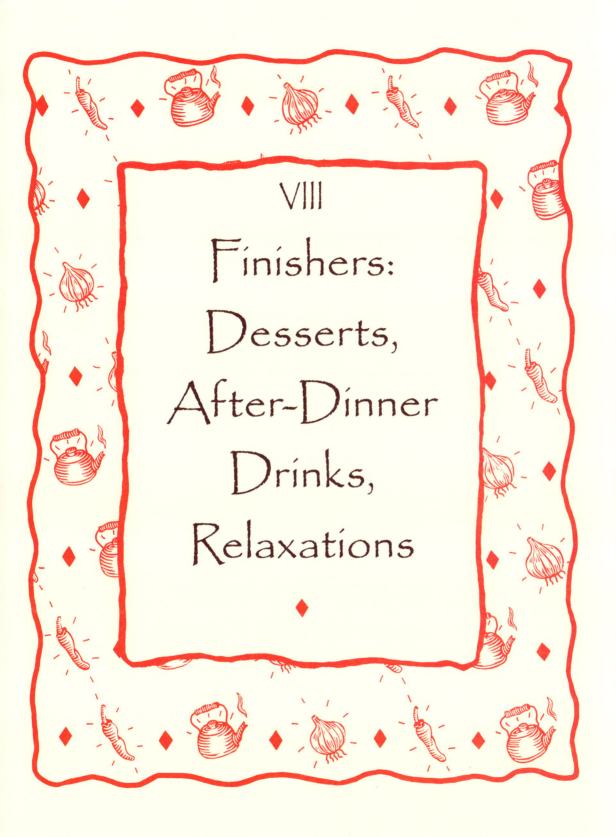

VIII

Finishers: Desserts, After-Dinner Drinks, Relaxations

Pralines

In the 1880s and '90s, my great-grandfather on my father's side operated a traveling circus up and down the border towns on both sides of the Rio Grande, the dividing line between Mexico and Texas. My great-grandfather was noted for his pralines, and his tamales, but it was the pralines that lured children of all ages inside the circus "walls."

This recipe may not be too different from the one my great-grandfather used those many years ago. He taught it to his son, Delfino, who in turn taught it to my father, Matt, Sr.

Makes 36 to 45 pralines

4 cups sugar	2 cups water
1/2 cup butter	4 cups broken pecan pieces (big pieces or halves)
2 (14 ounce) cans Borden's Eagle Brand condensed milk	

Bring all the ingredients except the pecans to a boil in a 5- to 6-quart heavy pot.

Once boiling, lower the heat to a frisky simmer. Do not stray far from the stove; the mixture will foam over the sides of the pot for the next 20 to 25 minutes. Continue to whisk down the foam with a heavy metal whisk, until the foaming settles and no longer overflows.

Continue to cook at a frisky simmer for 45 minutes to 1 hour. Do not stop cooking until the praline mixture has solidified enough to make several soft balls. To see if the praline mixture has solidified enough, drop 1/4 teaspoon of the hot candy into a cup of cold water. Let it sit in the water for about 30 seconds, then try to form a soft ball with it. Until you can form a ball, the mixture is not ready. Once ready, add the pecans, stirring them into the candy thoroughly.

On a table, butter a 3- to 4-foot piece of butcher paper (aluminum foil is okay, in a pinch). The candy will be too hot to touch. With one tablespoon, dip into the pot and remove a 1 1/2- to 2-inch patty, then use another spoon to scrape the "ball" of hot candy onto the butcher paper. Leave the balls of candy on the sheet to cool and harden, 30 to 45 minutes. When the candies are hard enough, pack them individually or together in air-tight plastic containers. They will keep for several weeks in the refrigerator.

Whiskey Pralines

Before you begin, I feel obligated to point out the 4 things you absolutely should never do while drinking: Never drive on public roads; sharpen your knives; mess with your guns; or make pralines. You'll burn yourself every time, if you don't watch out. In fact, use the whiskey at your own risk. Drugstore cowboys may substitute brandy.

Makes 36 to 45 pralines

4 cups sugar	2 tablespoons Jack Daniel's whiskey (other brands at your own risk)
1/2 cup butter	3/4 teaspoon vanilla extract
2 (14-ounce) cans Borden's Eagle Brand condensed milk	4 cups broken pecan pieces (big pieces or halves)
2 cups water	

In a 5- to 6-quart heavy pot, bring the sugar, butter, milk, and water to a boil. Once boiling, lower the heat to a frisky simmer. Do not stray far from the stove; the mixture will foam over the sides of the pot for the next 20 to 25 minutes. Continue to whisk down the foam with a heavy metal whisk, until the foaming settles and no longer overflows.

Continue to cook at a frisky simmer for another 45 minutes to 1 hour. Do not stop cooking until the hot mixture has solidified enough to make several soft balls. To see if the mixture has solidified enough, drop 1/4 teaspoon of the hot candy into a cup of cold water. Let it sit in the water for about 30 seconds, then try to form a soft ball with it. Until you can form a ball, the mixture is not ready. Once ready, add the whiskey, vanilla, and pecans, stirring them into the candy thoroughly.

On a table, butter 3 to 4 feet of butcher paper (aluminum foil is okay, in a pinch). The candy will be too hot to touch. With a tablespoon, dip into the pot and remove a 1 1/2- to 2-inch patty, then use another spoon to scrape the "ball" of hot candy onto the butcher paper. Leave the balls of candy on the sheet to cool and harden, 30 to 45 minutes. When the candies are hard enough, pack them individually or together in air-tight plastic containers. They will keep for several weeks in the refrigerator.

Kahlúa Pralines

Many praline recipes call for syrup, or a touch of Karo, or baking soda. I don't know why. You don't need that extra stuff, if you follow my recipes.

Makes 36 to 45 pralines

4 cups sugar

1/2 cup butter

2 (14 ounce) cans Borden's Eagle Brand condensed milk

2 cups freshly brewed coffee

2 tablespoons brandy

3/4 teaspoon vanilla extract

1 1/2 ounces Hershey's unsweetened baking chocolate, cut up

4 cups broken pecan pieces (big pieces or halves)

Bring the sugar, butter, milk, and coffee to a boil in a 5- to 6-quart heavy pot.

Once boiling, lower the heat to a frisky simmer. Do not stray far from the stove; the mixture will foam over the sides of the pot for the next 20 to 25 minutes. Continue to whisk down the foam with a heavy metal whisk until the foaming settles and no longer overflows.

Continue to cook at a frisky simmer for another 45 minutes to 1 hour. Do not stop cooking until the hot mixture has solidified enough to make several soft balls. To see if the mixture has solidified enough, drop 1/4 teaspoon of the hot candy into a cup of cold water. Let the candy sit in the water for about 30 seconds, then try to form a soft ball with it. Until you can form a ball, the mixture is not ready. Once ready, add the brandy, vanilla, baking chocolate, and pecans, stirring them into the candy thoroughly.

On a table, butter 3 to 4 feet of butcher paper (aluminum foil is okay, in a pinch). The candy will be too hot to touch. With a tablespoon, dip into the pot and remove a 1 1/2- to 2-inch patty, then use another spoon to scrape the "ball" of hot candy onto the butcher paper. Leave the balls of candy on the sheet to cool and harden, 30 to 45 minutes. When the candies are hard enough, pack them individually or together in air-tight plastic containers. They will keep for several weeks in the refrigerator.

Whiskey Sauce with Fruit

My parents and I were catering a party at the LBJ Ranch in Johnson City one summer. I was 15 years old, and I had, on occasion, already sampled whiskey. Lyndon Johnson was Vice-President of the United States, and so had he.

I was always in awe of LBJ and Lady Bird and all of the politicians and friends they had over. One day I was helping Mr. Johnson get something from the house when he asked, "Little Matt, you drink whiskey?"

I tried not to look too surprised, and I tried to sound confident when I answered, "Sure."

He sorta wrinkled his eyes at me, like they were smiling, and he said, "Want some Jack Daniel's?"

He reached into a cabinet and pulled out a bottle that had "Jack Daniel's Green" written on the label. I thought it was a joke. I'd heard of Jack Daniel's, all right, but nothing green. I took my chances and said, "Sure."

He poured me some on the rocks. I threw it down my throat, and LBJ just snickered and said to a secret service agent, "Give him another, with Coke." Well, I threw that one down, too.

I've been drinking Jack Daniel's Green ever since. I figure if the Vice-President of the United States says a drink is okay by him, then you owe it to your country to keep doing it.

Here's a kinder, gentler way to enjoy Jack Daniel's. I'm almost certain Lyndon would approve, whether you use the Green or not.

Makes 4 to 6 servings (about 3/4 cup sauce)

1/2 cup butter	1/2 teaspoon vanilla extract
1/2 cup Jack Daniel's whiskey	1 1/2 cups of your favorite fresh fruit (pineapple, strawberries, peaches, or apples) sliced or coarsely chopped
1 cup sugar	
Juice from 1 fresh lemon	

Melt the butter over low heat. In a bowl, whisk the whiskey, sugar, lemon, and vanilla until the sugar starts to dissolve. Pour the liquid into the pan with the butter. Stir and allow the sauce to simmer on low heat for 2 to 3 minutes, until it is smooth.

Leave $1/4$ cup of the sauce in the same skillet and reserve the rest. Add $1/2$ cup of the fresh fruit to the skillet. Gently simmer the combination until the fruit is warm and soft.

For each serving, always use $1/4$ cup of sauce for $1/2$ cup of fruit; or, learn to adapt the formula for your own tastes.

Optional:
- Substitute your favorite rum or brandy for the whiskey.

Serving Suggestions:
- Spoon this topping over angel food cake.
- Spoon it over vanilla ice cream (it's the best).
- Use it as a sauce for your favorite pie or crepe.

Sopaipillas

Sopaipillas get real popular around the Christmas and New Year's holidays. It's one of those aromas that really excites your little ol' taste buds.

When I was a boy, my granny couldn't make 'em fast enough. I'd gobble up so many sopaipillas that I'd have to go lay down and pat my stomach for an hour, just so I could soften it up for one or two more.

Makes 12 to 14 sopaipillas

2 cups flour	1 cup whole milk
2 teaspoons baking powder	1/4 cup sugar
2 teaspoons salt	1/2 teaspoon ground cinnamon
1/4 cup vegetable oil, plus additional for deep frying	

In a bowl, mix the flour, baking powder, and salt, then thoroughly mix in 1/4 cup of the oil. Heat the milk to lukewarm (not too hot), then add it to the flour mixture. Knead well for 2 to 3 minutes.

Roll the flour into one big ball—about the size of a grapefruit. Cover it, and allow it to rest at room temperature for at least 30 minutes (2 hours is best). Knead the dough one more time for 1 or 2 minutes.

Form the dough into balls roughly 1 1/2 inches in diameter. On a floured board, roll out the balls into circles as thin as possible.

To a skillet, add enough vegetable oil to come halfway up the sides and heat to 375°. Carefully place the sopaipillas one at a time into the skillet, and fry for about 1 minute per side, or until the sopaipillas are golden brown.

Drain the sopaipillas on paper towels.

Mix the sugar and cinnamon together. Sprinkle the sweet mix over the sopaipillas and serve hot.

Matt Martinez's Culinary Frontier

Serving Suggestions:

+ Eat sopaipillas as they are.
+ Eat them with your favorite ice cream.
+ They're great with Fried Peaches (page 117).
+ Add some honey and butter on top.

Matt's Fresh Sweet and Sour Mix

This is a real winner in margaritas, sangrias, and as a Tom Collins mix.

Makes 1 quart

- 1 cup freshly squeezed lime or lemon juice
- 1 cup sugar

Pour the lime juice and sugar into a 1-quart container. Fill it to the top with water. Stir until the sugar has dissolved. Refrigerate (no more than 3 or 4 days), freeze, or use immediately.

I'm-Not-Lying-This-Time Margarita

Margaritas are not so much an after-dinner drink as a drink that perks the taste buds for what's to come. This particular one is a favorite "before dinner" and "during" dinner cocktail at Matt's No Place in Dallas.

I've been asked how this could be a margarita when it contains no tequila. Well, have one and tell me whether I'm lying this time or not.

Makes 1 drink

For the Rim (Good for 6 to 8 Drinks):

1/4 teaspoon cayenne pepper

1 package presweetened orange Kool-Aid

Juice from 1 fresh lime

For Each Drink:

1 lime wedge

1 1/2 ounces brandy

Crushed ice

Matt's Fresh Sweet and Sour Mix (see preceding recipe)

Mix the cayenne pepper and Kool-Aid. Rim a 10-ounce martini, highball, or margarita glass by dipping it first into the lime juice, then into the Kool-Aid mixture.

Squeeze the lime wedge and leave it in the glass. Add the brandy, and fill the glass to the top with crushed ice. Fill the glass to its rim with sweet and sour mix, stir, and serve.

South Austin Margarita

This was the first margarita recipe at Matt's El Rancho, when we initially got our liquor license. If you like margaritas, I'm reasonably certain you'll find that it has nicely weathered the test of time.

Makes 1 drink

For the Rim (Good for 6 to 8 Drinks):

Juice from 1 fresh lime   Kosher salt

For Each Drink:

Crushed ice   1/2 ounce Cointreau

1 1/2 ounces Sauza Conmemorativo   1 lime wedge
tequila

Matt's Fresh Sweet and Sour
Mix (page 226)

Rim a 10-ounce margarita glass by dipping it into the lime juice, then the kosher salt.

Fill the glass to the rim with crushed ice. Add the tequila. Fill the glass to its rim with the sweet and sour mix. Add the splash of cointreau.

Squeeze the lime wedge into the glass and stir the drink well before serving.

Matt Martinez, Sr., enjoying a margarita on the patio of Matt's El Rancho in Austin

Matt's 80-Calorie Margarita

This combination of NutraSweet, lime juice, and water, mixed with tequila, will quench your thirst without piling on too many calories.

Some of my buddies and I prefer to use this margarita as an antidepressant for fishing. We carry it around in gallon jugs. If we don't catch any fish, we go to the jug. If we catch a bunch of fish and have to clean them, we go to the jug.

It's also good for snake scares: If a water moccasin scares hell out of you, go immediately to your jug.

Makes 1 drink

For the Rim (Good for 6 to 8 Drinks):

Juice from 1 fresh lime   Kosher salt

For Each Drink:

3/4	ounce freshly squeezed lime juice	2	ounces water
1	package NutraSweet or Equal		Crushed ice
1	ounce Sauza Conmemorativo tequila	1	lime slice

Rim a 10-ounce margarita or martini glass by dipping it into the lime juice and then (very lightly) the kosher salt.

Pour the freshly squeezed lime juice into the glass and stir in the NutraSweet or Equal. Add the tequila and water.

Fill the glass to the rim with crushed ice. Stir. Garnish it with the lime slice, and serve.

Matt's Magic Sangria

This sangria has a pleasantly tart taste that goes great with spicy foods. It's actually more than an after-dinner drink. It's a before, during, or after drink—all 3 if you're not driving.

Makes one 2-quart pitcher

For Each Glass Rim:

Juice of 1 fresh lime   Brown sugar

For a 2-Quart Pitcher Drink:

1 quart red wine	1 lime wedge per glass
1 quart freshly squeezed orange juice	Crushed ice
1 pint peach or apricot brandy	1 orange slice per glass

Rub the rim of a 10-ounce martini, margarita, or sangria glass with lime juice, then dip the rim in brown sugar. Pour the red wine, orange juice, and brandy in the pitcher. Squeeze the lime wedge into the glass, stir, and fill the glass to the rim with crushed ice. Fill with sangria and garnish with the orange slice.

Prairie Mary Cocktail Mix

This mix is particularly relevant to the next two recipes, the Prairie Mary and the "Hello!"

Makes one 2-quart pitcher

1 quart tomato juice	1/4 cup Worcestershire sauce
1/2 teaspoon peppercorns	1 tablespoon salt, plus extra, to taste
1/2 teaspoon mustard seed	1 whole jalapeño chile pepper, or 1/4 cup chopped pickled jalapeño with juice
1 cup coarsely chopped white onions	
1 cup coarsely chopped celery	
1/4 cup fresh lemon juice	

Combine 1 cup of the tomato juice with the other ingredients in the container of a blender, and blend on low for 1 minute.

In a large pitcher, combine the blender mixture with the remaining tomato juice. Stir it well, and adjust the salt to your taste.

The mix is best served chilled.

Optional:
◆ For another twist, add 1/4 cup chopped fresh cilantro, loosely packed, at the beginning.

Prairie Mary

This is the sister of Bloody Mary. Some of you may have seen Bloody Mary in airports, before early morning flights. Prairie Mary never flies, but she can sure get your feet off the ground.

Makes 10 to 15 servings

For the Rim Salt:

1/2 cup salt of choice	1/2 teaspoon cayenne pepper
1/2 teaspoon white pepper	1/4 teaspoon dried thyme

For Each Cocktail:

10–15 Lime wedges	1 cup vodka (I prefer Ketel One)
2-quart pitcher Prairie Mary Mix (see preceding recipe)	

Blend the rim salt and use it to rim half of each glass. Roll the lime wedges in the remaining rim salt. Squeeze a lime wedge into each glass.

Combine the Prairie Mary Mix and the vodka. Stir and pour into salt-rimmed glasses filled with crushed ice.

Optional:

- Garnish each drink with a celery stick.
- The rim salt recipe is also good on Bloody Marys and "Hello!"

"Hello!"

I gave this drink its name because that's the first thing out of your mouth once you take a healthy gulp.

Those times when everyone in camp is just waking up and still sleepy-eyed, I make a few "Hellos!"

And off we go.

They're also good "appetizers" for margaritas.

Makes 1 drink

1 ounce tequila

1 ounce Prairie Mary Mix, chilled (page 231)

Pinch of rim salt (see preceding recipe)

1 lime wedge

In a small, chilled on-the-rocks glass, combine the tequila and chilled cocktail mix.

Hold the drink in your left hand. Put a pinch of salt on a lime wedge. Smile at your guests (if alone, smile at yourself in a mirror). Bite the lime, slam the drink, and immediately you should hear the sound of your own voice shouting "Hello!"

Tequila Sour

My favorite actor is Lee Marvin. By chance, he strolled into Matt's El Rancho in Austin one afternoon and we really hit it off.

He said he had some time to kill while waiting on a couple of friends. For starters, Mr. Marvin sucked down a chile relleno with shrimp, explaining that he ate it so fast because he didn't want to embarrass me. Then he asked me to make him another one just like that.

After he ate that one, too, I led him through the kitchen and into a private room in the back of the restaurant, where we spent the next 3 hours discussing the pros and cons of drinking.

"I drank so much one night," he told me in that gravelly voice of his, "I couldn't drink anything else until I got up the next morning."

I asked if he would like for me to make a pitcher of margaritas. He slowly shook his head from side to side and said, "Can't do it. I got a bet going that I won't drink a margarita for an entire month."

I grabbed some fresh lime, some Triple Sec, and tequila, and I rimmed a glass with a little salt.

Mr. Marvin curiously eyed me and said, "Hold on there, that's not a margarita, is it?"

"Nope," I assured.

That afternoon, I introduced Lee Marvin to Tequila Sours. I do not know if he won his bet, but he wasn't about to lose on my account. We spent the next couple of hours drinking tequila sours, until his two friends showed up.

Except for the times I've had the pleasure of being in the delightful company of Julia Child, that visit from Lee Marvin may have been the most fun I've ever had with a celebrity.

Makes 1 drink

For the Rim (Good for 6 to 8 Drinks):

Juice of 1 fresh lime   Kosher salt

For Each Drink:

- 1 cup ice
- 1 ounce Sauza Conmemorativo tequila (silver, not gold)

- 1 ounce Triple Sec (DeKuyper is best)
- 1 ounce fresh lemon juice

Rim a chilled 10-ounce margarita or martini glass by dipping it into the lime juice and then (very lightly) the kosher salt.

Add the ice and liquids to a shaker, and shake 6 times (not too much, not too little). Pour the drink into the chilled glass.

Bushwhacker Lemonade

Let's say you are hosting a party, and everybody's standing around tongue-tied. Maybe they don't know each other. You try and try, but nobody is loosening up. Here's what I usually serve to get everything rolling.

This drink bushwhacks you because you can't taste the vodka. You feel like you're enjoying a cool lemonade when all of a sudden you get bright-eyed, there's more color in your cheeks, and your smile muscles start working overtime.

Happy days are here again.

Warning: Severe craziness exhibited in my presence—by others, of course—force me to insist that under no circumstances should you make Bushwhackers with tequila.

Makes 4 to 6 servings (1 pitcher)

8 ounces vodka (Ketel One is best; you can't taste it)	Ice cubes
1 cup sugar	1 slice fresh peach or Granny Smith apple per drink, peeled, as a garnish
1 cup fresh lemon juice	
Cold water	

In a 2-quart pitcher, mix the vodka with the sugar and lemon juice, and stir vigorously. Fill the pitcher to the top with the cold water.

Fill each glass with ice cubes, pour on the Bushwhacker Lemonade, garnish with the peach or apple slice, and drink up.

Optional:

◆ To make Bushwhacker Lemonade No. 2, use bourbon instead of vodka, and garnish with naval orange slices.

◆ For Bushwhacker Lemonade No. 3, use rum, and garnish with a slice of fresh pineapple.

◆ For more tartness, use extra lemon wedges for squeezing into the glasses.

◆ Should you decide to perk the taste buds even further, use this Bushwhacker Spicy Rim mix:

4   tablespoons presweetened Kool-Aid (lemon, lime, or orange)

1   teaspoon salt

1   teaspoon cayenne pepper

Thoroughly mix the Kool-Aid, salt, and pepper. Before putting the ice into the glass, moisten the rim with the fruit of your choice, or with a wet finger, and dip the glass rim into the spicy mixture.

Wine Suggestions

Ley Jaynes and Walter Walsh, my neighbors at Grailey's Fine Wines, were kind enough to pour their years of wine wisdom into this segment. Before moving in the spring of '97, Grailey's was next door to Matt's Rancho Martinez and Matt's No Place, in Dallas.

When it comes to looking for a wine to enjoy with Tex-Mex and other spicier dishes, Ley and Walter throw up one cautionary red-flare warning:

Do not drink a heavy, highly acidic wine, such as a Cabernet Sauvignon, with these meals. Go with something sweeter and fruitier. A heavy, smoky wine only exaggerates the spices in the food, rather than complementing them.

With spicier dishes, select a wine that will act as a cleanser on the palate. That should give your taste buds a break from the spices, before you go back for more fire.

For main courses that include jalapeño or chile pepper flavoring, go with a Pinot Noir, or a lighter, fruitier Zinfandel, or a Barbera d'Alba from Italy.

For spicy chicken or queso dishes, such white wines as California Chenin Blanc, France's Vouvray or Muscadet, or the German-graped Gewürztraminer go well.

Overall, for any spicy food, you can't go wrong with a Blanc de Noir or any good rosé sparkling wine.

For 30/30 Duck, go with a full-bodied Merlot, Zinfandel, or Pinot Noir.

For steaks, Cabernet Sauvignon is the old standby. Red Bordeaux and Chianti are also good.

For after-dinner wines and dessert wines, Grailey's gang suggests a Late Harvest Zinfandel, which is fairly sweet and fruity, or a good port. Late bottled vintage ports offer better enjoyment than the earlier vintage ports for drinking now rather than for storing.

The regions of Mexico have not produced much in the way of fine wine. Argentina and Chile are the up-and-coming wine-producing countries in South America. But, unless you are looking to complement a milder dish, such as a baked fish with little seasoning, go with the lighter varieties.

And if you are about to dive head first into Matt's Competition Chili or some other big-time bowl of red?

I say store the wine.

As an appetizer, have a margarita. With the chili, pop open a few bottles of cold beer.

The Wonderful World of After-Dinner Cigars

If you're going to enjoy a fine after-dinner smoke, do not be misled by preconceived notions.

They used to say you should smoke the cigar that goes best with

Matt Jr. (left) enjoys a cigar and fine wine with his manager, Lizzie Ashworth, artist Rick Timmons, and singer Red Reynolds.

your face—skinny or fat, short or long. I say try several and go with what you enjoy.

I've had the pleasure of hosting many "cigar smokers" at my No Place restaurant in Dallas. I've also chewed on and smoked my share of cigars. Some were stogies. Some were heaven.

Cigars for Short Drives or When You're in a Rush

My favorite cigar for puddle-jumping and other quick hops is the Hemingway Short Story, a brand of the Dominican cigar Arturo Fuente. It's a twenty-one- or twenty-two-minute cigar, which is just about right if you're feeling rushed but still want a smoke. I prefer the light-wrapper. At Matt's No Place, we sell quite a few cigars, and we'd sell a great many more of these except they're too hard to get. I keep 'em for myself. I mean, there are some things you just don't share with your friends.

Cigars for Cognacs and Ports

My favorite drinking cigar is the Padron Delicias. It's a dark-wrapper cigar, but not too strong. It draws beautifully, and it's a long-cut tobacco that remains delicate from start to finish. Come to think of it, the Padron Delicias is good with any kind of drinking.

Cigars for Longer Stints

I've made the 200-mile drive from Dallas to Austin so often that sometimes it's hard for me to figure whether I'm coming or going. Whatever the direction, I go with Indios No. 2 Especial cigars. These Honduras beauties are smooth, long-lasting cigars with no bite. Dallas to Austin is a four-cigar drive (two up, two back) with these babies.

IX

Cooking

Methods

◆

Smoking

I tip my hat to those of you who know your way around a smoker. Smoking is an art, as any serious rib eater will attest.

It's also a great way to do chicken, duck, fish, turkey, vegetables, and, of course, briskets and roasts.

Some Southwestern chefs prefer to smoke with mesquite wood. I like dry mesquite for grilling, but not for smoking. Mesquite is too intense, too dense, for smoking. It starves for oxygen too easily and leaves a bitter taste. Mesquite wood can be used in a pinch if it has been seasoned for at least a year. But even then, I prefer to remove all the bark, which contains much of the bitter taste.

I encourage the use of hickory, oak, pecan, or one of the fruit woods (apple, cherry, peach, for example). My favorites are pecan and hickory.

The best smokers come with instructions that detail their own unique qualities (such as how many minutes per pound is preferable for meat, fish, vegetables, and so on).

Grilling

Dry mesquite is best for grilling. I like to build my fire away from the grill and shovel in the coals, maintaining $1^1/_2$ to 2 inches of burning embers at the bottom of the grill.

Don't make the mistake of throwing the food on before the coals are hot enough. Allow roughly thirty minutes on nongas grills (ten to fifteen minutes for gas grills), or until the coals are burning evenly and have an ash coating.

For whole or larger pieces of chicken, ribs, fish, and vegetables, I try to keep the grill surface 16 to 20 inches above the flame.

For steaks, thin fillets (such as catfish), thin chicken strips or breasts, and kabobs, I prefer more heat and therefore like the grill 8 to 10 inches above the flame.

Experiment with your grill. If you find that the food is cooking too fast, simply move it farther from the major source of heat. But cooking on a grill is usually a matter of minutes.

Also, try not to spear your steaks too often with a pronged fork. All of those wonderful juices end up on the coals instead of in your mouth. Tongs avoid this problem.

Nor should you crowd the grill; give the food some air. Allow $^1/_2$ inch to an inch of room between each piece.

Index

Italicized page numbers indicate photographs